THE
WATER-SAVING
GARDEN

THE WATER-SAVING GARDEN

HOW TO GROW A GORGEOUS GARDEN WITH A LOT LESS WATER

Pam Penick

TEN SPEED PRESS
Berkeley

To those who see

contents

introduction

Water is easy to take for granted
in our country.

Gushing from the faucet at the touch of a lever or twist of a knob, the most
precious resource in the world—clean drinking water—gurgles into our
homes like magic. Our great-grandparents may have hand-pumped a well,
and their ancestors lugged buckets of water from the river. But we're so
accustomed to the convenience and availability of fresh water that we design
our homes and grade our property to shed water and then pay to pipe it
back in and spray it across our yards when rainfall is scarce—and often even
when it isn't. With a heedlessness born of cheap, plentiful water—a supply
many regions can no longer count on—we run our sprinklers automatically
and excessively, carpet our yards with thirsty lawn without regard to
climate, and let rainwater and irrigation run off our yards and driveways
into the street. This is madness. We must stop treating water as a disposable
commodity in our landscapes and gardens and conserve it like the precious,
limited resource it is.

The specter of drought, which has always haunted the American West,
Great Plains, and Southwest, has lately spurred widespread interest in
removing water-hogging lawns and an acceptance of drier gardens and
native plants. Even in the wetter parts of the country, particularly the
mid-Atlantic, Southeast, and Midwest, water conservation is increasingly
popular. Combined with a renewed national interest in living more
sustainably with less waste of our natural resources, water conservation—
and, more broadly, water management—is now a priority no matter
where one lives.

Baja fairy duster
(*Calliandra californica*)
adds color and lushness
to a desert garden.

A wooden panel painted by Reuben Muñoz illustrates the interconnectedness of nature and humans, with water essential to both.

This is not to say we must not water our gardens, and it's certainly not to say we must not *have* a garden. Planting a garden is a way of connecting with the natural rhythms of the seasons and with the earth itself. It's a deeply worthy endeavor that brings beauty into our lives and communities, offers islands of wildlife habitat amid acres of paved urban sprawl, and teaches us the slower virtues of patience and hope in a fast-paced, need-it-yesterday world. A garden is an expression of creativity, and the finest gardens are works of art that excite, delight, or move us. Gardens feed our bodies and our spirits. They soothe us when we're sick or sick at heart. Some can even accomplish that most miraculous feat of all: enticing our increasingly housebound children away from their computers and smartphones to trail their fingers in a pond, follow a butterfly's fluttering path, or explore a mysterious, winding path.

All gardens—except those consisting only of rocks—need water to live. Even cacti cannot live without water. So how do we reconcile our wish to conserve—or, for those of us in drought-plagued regions, our pressing *need* to conserve—this most essential resource with our desire for a garden, and more than that, for a beautiful garden?

We do it by changing the way we garden and by shifting our ideas of what a garden can be and should look like. Just as we've learned to reduce water use indoors by turning off the faucet while we brush our teeth, installing low-flow toilets and showerheads, and waiting until the dishwasher is full before running a load, we can take similar water-saving measures in our gardens. These include choosing plants well adapted to our climate, irrigating less often and more efficiently, and using water-permeable paving. In addition, we can design gardens that actively collect rainwater and eliminate wasteful runoff. We can even use artistic arrangements of rock and plants to satisfy our "sweet tooth" for water by evoking the idea of it. Now that's getting creative!

This book will show you that a water-saving garden can be so much more than just cacti or succulents, although certainly those can be beautiful too. A garden that sips instead of guzzles can be quite lush if planted with regionally appropriate plants. It's a matter of adjusting expectations of what a garden *should* be and creating a responsible garden in harmony with nature. It's about accepting the reality of one's climate and gardening accordingly. If you live in a dry-summer climate, acknowledge that your garden will not be as flowery then as in wetter seasons and forgo the thirsty bedding annuals or perennials. If your region is arid, replace the lawn (or at least most of it) with native plants that thrive on rainfall, with occasional irrigation to get through excessively dry periods. It's a commonsense approach with far-reaching impact and the added long-term benefits of saving you money and effort.

All it takes is a willingness to garden in tune with local conditions. This may take some experimentation as climate change alters our traditional weather patterns, causing more extreme weather events including flooding and drought, deep freezes and heat waves. But the payoff is a garden that adds value to your life and your community without the burden of guilt about water waste, a garden that is more likely to survive if water shortages mandate watering restrictions, and a garden that gives more than it takes.

We'll start in Part One by touring several inspiring water-saving gardens to see what's working, with particular attention to design ideas you can apply to your own yard.

In Part Two you'll get practical, DIY-friendly techniques for holding on to rainwater through grading of soil, rain barrels, rain gardens, and water-permeable paving. We'll discuss irrigation, how to decide whether it's needed, and how to water efficiently, and you'll get the dirt on improving your soil's ability to hold water. Shade structures and windbreaks can also make a difference in preserving soil moisture, so we'll explore various ways of blocking sun and wind.

Part Three is all about plants. We'll look at alternatives to the ubiquitous, thirsty lawn; how to group plants by watering needs, using native and adapted plants; and the best time of year to plant. Balcony and patio gardeners will appreciate a chapter devoted to saving water in container gardens.

In Part Four we'll explore creative ways of adding the illusion of watery abundance in a garden. From dry creeks to stream-like mosaics to contemporary, colored-glass "rivers," squeezing water from stone has never been so fun. Like stone, certain plants evoke the idea of water through a cascading or spraying form. In addition, ancient dry-garden traditions like Japanese Zen gardens and Moorish gardens have much to teach us about gardening with less water, and we'll see what can be reinterpreted for today's gardens.

Part Five gets you started with a list of 101 plants with drought tolerance for gardens across the country. You'll find a variety of trees, shrubs, perennials, groundcovers, and more, with brief descriptions and growing information to help you make the right choices for your climate and your garden's specific conditions.

part one

DRINK UP
the beauty & ingenuity
of a water-saving garden

Do you love cacti? Great! Nothing sips water more daintily than these spiny desert plants. But if you hate cacti (and let's face it, cactus plants tend to inspire either love or loathing), you'll be relieved to know that water-saving gardens, even in arid regions, may contain no cacti at all. Imagine a garden alight with deep-rooted dryland grasses, native and adapted shrubs and trees, seasonal wildflowers that go dormant in dry months, small succulents, woody lilies like agave and yucca, silvery or gray-green groundcovers, and various hairy-, waxy-, or tiny-leaved plants superbly adapted to hot, dry conditions.

In a dry strip along the street, water-thrifty plants like whale's tongue agave (*Agave ovatifolia*) flourish.

Maybe you don't live in a hot, dry climate, but you still want a garden that saves water. First, good for you! Daily watering, even in a temperate climate, is wasteful and costly. Instead of fussy plants that need regular watering, fill your garden with those that thrive on natural rainfall and need supplemental watering only when it's abnormally dry. If you want to grow dry-loving plants, mound up your garden beds for quick drainage. Or go the opposite route and dig a shallow depression in which to plant a rain garden.

Perhaps you'd like to save water in a particularly drought- or heat-stressed area of your yard—the dried-out strip along the street or driveway, a south-facing slope, or sun-blasted patches of lawn, for example—but still want to grow some of your favorite thirstier plants. This is one of the principles of xeriscaping, or gardening in a way that conserves water: group plants with similar water needs together, and keep thirstier plants close to the house and the hose for easier maintenance. It's a tried-and-true way to cut back on watering without feeling you must sacrifice all of your favorites.

drink up the beauty & ingenuity of a water-saving garden

The point is, there's no one "right way" to plant a garden that saves water. Rather, it's about planting thoughtfully, using plants that can subsist on natural rainfall or judicious supplemental watering, grouping plants by water need, and saving higher-water plants you love for small areas where you can most easily enjoy and water them.

Plant choice is often the first thing that comes to mind to gardeners who want to save water. We readily reconsider our plants but often overlook other opportunities to save water, like our hardscape choices. Thoughtfully designed hardscape—the manmade, nonliving parts of our gardens, like paths, patios, decks, walls, and other constructions—is, by nature, a water-saving device. After all, paths and seating areas never need a drink of water. Retaining walls, which create level terraces on slopes and hillsides, give runoff a chance to soak in and saturate the soil rather than sheeting downhill like water off a dry sponge. A water-saving garden may make use of increased areas of hardscape, with the added bonus of creating inviting spaces for you and your guests to enjoy the garden.

You can also get artistic in the pursuit of a water-saving garden. Dry creeks, swirling mosaics of river stones, cascading plants—all can be used to evoke the idea of water in a dry garden. Japanese Zen gardens are a classic example of this, with raked gravel that represents the sea dotted by boulder "islands." Incorporate some of these ancient, dry-garden design motifs into your own garden to create an illusion of water without turning on the hose.

Now let's tour seven inspirational water-saving gardens, which will get you thinking about ideas for your own spaces. As you absorb design lessons from these gardens, keep in mind that while plant choice is highly dependent on local conditions, design concepts are universal. No matter where you live, you can put ideas about hardscape, berming, terracing, plant grouping, water collection, or anything else to work in your garden, while selecting plants based on your local climate. And now, let's tour!

dry-garden journey to a courtyard oasis

Lakewood Garden, Austin, Texas

A textural explosion of flowering grasses, feathery trees, and spherical, shimmering yuccas greets visitors to this suburban Austin home. Designed by landscape architect Curt Arnette of Sitio Design, the garden replaced a featureless lawn so large that all it lacked was a county courthouse in the center to complete the village green effect. Meeting the goals of reducing water use and adding privacy, this water-thrifty garden also succeeds in

Above: The rosy blooms of Gulf muhly (*Muhlenbergia capillaris*) soften and color a gray-green garden of spikier plants.

Below left: Gravelly berms add interest and drainage.

Below right: A modern water feature leads the way into the front courtyard.

creating a garden journey. Broad decomposed-granite paths curve past bermed, gravelly planting beds of bold-leaved palms and fluffy grasses, flowering perennials and spiky agaves, leading visitors on an exploratory amble toward the front door.

On the formerly flat lot, limestone boulders, loosely arranged and half buried, edge broad, mounded planting beds. These berms provide excellent drainage for dry-soil loving plants, elevating them above clay hardpan and preventing rainwater from swamping their roots during Texas gullywashers. They also sculpt the lot, adding height to the planting beds through which the gravel paths wind.

The naturalistic style of the outer garden segues into a more contemporary design inside a fenced courtyard garden that leads to the home's entry. Rust-colored steel-mesh panels and an arbor provide enclosure, deer-proofing, and a sense of privacy without obstructing views or breezes. A rectangular pool at the gate acts as a wellspring for a concrete rill, which flows through the fence and spills into a circular pond in the courtyard. A recirculating water feature like this can make a big impact without using much water—certainly not as much as a thirsty lawn would—and can function as a dry-garden oasis. The rill directs visitors through a courtyard garden filled with low-water plants and toward the house.

Within the courtyard, plants are relegated to perimeter beds, making it easy to water them on a drip line and leaving the center open for decomposed-granite paving—negative space that in a thirstier garden might be sodded with lawn. Decomposed granite yields the same openness but never needs watering.

Like a sparkling waterfall, silver ponyfoot (*Dichondra argentea*) spills over the edge of a raised bed of agaves and yuccas, creating a sense of water even amid dry-loving plants.

The back garden is laid out in a similar fashion to the front, with broad gravel paths—more hardscape means less watering—curving through bermed and naturalistically planted beds. Shade-tolerant plants take the place of sun-lovers under the trees.

Clockwise from top left: Xeric plants edge the path leading to a gravel courtyard.

A simple circular pool is fed by a concrete rill running alongside the path.

Casual gravel paths curve through a shade garden behind the house.

Silver ponyfoot cascades over steel edging like a waterfall.

drink up the beauty & ingenuity of a water-saving garden

The Zen design disguises a concrete floor with gravel and decking while still allowing water to move away from the house.

zen inspiration for a concrete jungle

Ted and Nancy Dobson Garden, Eugene, Oregon

Wall-to-wall concrete, channeled down the middle to funnel water runoff away from the house, originally offered a prison-yard ambience for Ted and Nancy Dobson, the owners of this Eugene, Oregon, home. Outside views were of bleak paving, a sparsely planted bed atop a retaining wall, and the house next door towering over theirs.

From such an unpromising beginning unfolded a remarkable transformation. Rebecca Sams and Buell Steelman of Mosaic Gardens were tasked by the owners with creating a welcoming garden without removing the concrete paving, which had to remain due to drainage concerns. Undaunted, Sams and Steelman found inspiration in the dry-garden tradition of Japanese temple gardens, which at their simplest include only a few carefully sited boulders and raked gravel. They hit on the idea of layering over the concrete with river rock, stepping stones, and decking in the style of a Japanese Zen garden.

It was a brilliant solution. Local river rock in hues of gray, ivory, and taupe slows but does not impede the movement of water across the property, allowing it to flow safely away from the home's foundation. At the same time, it completely masks the concrete paving with a textural, natural-looking surface. As in Zen gardens, its rippled expanse creates the illusion of water; the gravel represents the sea, or perhaps, in this small garden, a pond. Traversing the gravel, a winding stepping-stone path is set high, as if over the surface of the pond, adding to the illusion. Along the way, bamboo screens enticingly frame views of bonsai-like potted pines, a stone lantern, and a vessel water feature, even as they hide the home's heat pump from view of anyone sitting on the deck.

The floor of the garden is, in the Zen garden tradition, sparingly planted, with only a few large potted conifers and grasses clustered near the deck and framed by the bamboo screens. Watered on a drip system (the irrigation tubing is hidden under the river rock), the minimalist arrangement gives the tiny garden room to breathe and shows how effective a dry-garden design can be, even in a relatively rainy climate.

Evergreen shrubs, trees, and grasses in varying shades of steely blue, chartreuse, burgundy, and emerald green weave a tapestry of rich color in the sloping bed atop the wall, effectively screening the neighboring house and creating a beautiful view from the ipe wood deck, which offers space for dining or relaxing—and of course never needs to be watered.

Left: A vessel water feature with a bent-pipe fountain puts a modern spin on the traditional Zen-garden bamboo fountain and stone basin.

Right: Chunky stepping stones appear to float across the gravel, reinforcing the watery illusion created by the pebbly floor.

drink up the beauty & ingenuity of a water-saving garden

This page: A large gravel patio extends the home's outdoor living space.

Opposite above: Native desert plants don't need a lot of water and add architectural beauty against colored walls.

Opposite below: Gravel patios are both economical and water permeable.

embracing the desert for outdoor living

Quartz Mountain Garden, Paradise Valley, Arizona

Until relatively recently, desert dwellers in the Southwest often planted in denial of the desert, installing water-sucking lawns and Mediterranean-style landscaping heavy on Italian cypress, palms, and other heat-tolerant exotics. While rugged mountain views were treasured, indigenous plants were scorned as thorny weeds, unworthy of a garden setting. Sprinklers ran daily. As Phoenix landscape architect Steve Martino describes them, these were landscapes on life support. His mission for the past thirty years has been to pull the plug and create gardens that won't die if the water is shut off and that "celebrate where we live rather than make apologies for it."

That philosophy attracted the owners of a modernist 1960s home in Paradise Valley, Arizona, who were in the midst of a remodel and expansion. They asked Martino to create a garden with outdoor entertaining and play spaces for their growing family. Martino added a covered patio for shade and extended window views out into gravel and concrete-paver patios planted with sculptural native plants framed by richly colored walls.

drink up the beauty & ingenuity of a water-saving garden

With contemporary lines that reflect the home's architecture, the large gravel sitting area just off the covered patio significantly increases the home's entertaining space. Adirondack chairs cluster convivially around an outdoor fireplace that warms chilly desert evenings. Shaped like tall, green pipe cleaners, spindly ocotillo (*Fouquieria splendens*) contrasts with the chunky, salad-plate-sized pads of prickly pear (*Opuntia* spp.) against a tomato-red wall. Along with using native desert plants instead of thirsty exotics, choosing gravel instead of lawn to floor this space saves a tremendous amount of water.

Still, water is not banished from the garden but given selective prominence, focused for impact. At the covered patio's edge, a shelf fountain built into the wall spills into a rectangular pool cut into the floor. Lawn isn't completely banished either but shrunk into a defined rectangle, giving the kids a place to play—an extravagance made more affordable by a water-thrifty design throughout the remaining garden.

The majority of the property is landscaped in harmony with the desert. Southwestern natives predominate, but well-adapted exotics earn their keep too. Native palo verde trees flower butter-yellow in spring, looking like forsythia on steroids. Toothy agaves add sword-leaved structure. Spiny prickly pear and hairy white cacti glow with captured sunlight. Long-armed, smooth-skinned aloes send up spires of tubular, hummingbird-attracting blooms each spring, and lantana flowers pumpkin-orange nearly all year.

Enclosing and framing different sections of the garden, colored stucco and rusty steel walls are the garden's year-round backbone. Their shady sides create microclimates for plants that need a little protection from the sun; their sunny sides retain heat and offer some winter protection to tender plants. Above all they bring the rugged landscape down to human scale, even as they frame views of knife-edged, rocky mountains in the distance. This garden certainly celebrates the desert rather than apologizing for it.

Check dams made of rock excavated on-site help prevent runoff when it rains.

holding on to every drop of rain

Christine Ten Eyck Garden, Austin, Texas

When landscape architect Christine Ten Eyck returned to Austin, Texas, after decades working in Arizona, she was excited by the possibilities of making gardens in a place that gets an average of 33 inches of annual rainfall compared to Phoenix's 8 inches. But all that extra rain is for naught, she observed with dismay at her new home, if it simply runs off your property into the street.

She and her husband inherited an expansive, sloping St. Augustine lawn and a long, circular driveway that shed water like a dry sponge during heavy rains. Dozens of mature live oaks provided cooling shade, but the driveway that delivered cars right to the front windows of their home was not so welcome. With a twofold goal of eliminating the parking-lot view

and holding every drop of rainwater that fell on the property, she ripped out the circular drive (a new, narrower driveway along the edge of the lot serves the couple's needs) *and* the lawn and built check dams in broad arcs across the front yard.

Check dams are small dams that slow the flow of water during rainstorms. Unlike terracing, they don't require resculpting the soil or building sturdy retaining walls. To avoid disturbing the root systems of the live oaks, Ten Eyck opted not to do a lot of earth moving or terracing of her sloping lot, which drops about eight feet between the house and the street. Instead, the check dams, constructed of stacked limestone and backfilled with topsoil excavated from a sunken patio in her back garden, provide a gentler solution. Like embracing arms, they curve in low arcs to collect runoff and give it time to soak into the soil. Ten Eyck built bands of them across the lot, giving the live oaks a wide berth, and in the soil pockets planted native understory trees and shade-tolerant perennials, grasses, woody lilies, and groundcovers.

A broad decomposed-granite path, six to eight feet wide, winds through the garden from the street to the front door, offering a journey through a native-plant garden that resembles a dappled woodland, with pockets of sunlight that allow for a small vegetable garden. A hidden patio with benches of limestone boulders is screened from the street by feathery clouds of bamboo muhly (*Muhlenbergia dumosa*).

Where cars once blocked garden views in front of the house, Ten Eyck gave the house some breathing room with clean-lined concrete pavers and gravel. Steel risers create shallow terracing for steps and a raised bed—essentially an extension of the front porch. With low, foundation-softening plants in the raised bed, like Mexican feathergrass (*Nassella tenuissima*), purple oxalis (*Oxalis triangularis*), and squid agave (*Agave bracteosa*), the owners now enjoy an unobstructed view into the garden from inside their home.

And now when it rains, water doesn't run off the property into the street. Instead, it's slowed and held by the check dams and soaks in to nourish the oaks and understory plants, making the garden not just more welcoming but smarter and harder working as well.

Clockwise from top left: An S-shaped check dam skirts mature trees and creates a sinuous line.

Native perennials and grasses border a path made of decomposed-granite.

Pavers set in pea gravel offer clean, modern lines and water permeability.

A front-yard seating area feels private thanks to tall grasses and shrubs.

painting a dry slope with color

Gravel Garden at Chanticleer, Wayne, Pennsylvania

Chanticleer, a public "pleasure garden" in Wayne, Pennsylvania, is celebrated for its inventive plant combinations and playful design sensibility. Perhaps surprisingly for this part of the country, it also contains an inspirational example of a dry garden. Planted on a long, sunny slope, the Gravel Garden is a colorful quilt of flowering perennials, self-sowing annuals, seasonal bulbs, and spreading groundcovers, threaded with ribbons of feathery grasses and accented with a few cold-tolerant yuccas.

Originally formally terraced and planted with thirsty, demanding roses, the slope was completely transformed in the 1990s, during Chanticleer's transition from private home to public garden. Today this naturalistic dry garden needs little to no supplemental water. Mediterranean plants and dry-loving natives take in stride the sun-baked, fast-draining conditions imposed on them by the steep, open hillside. Rounded gravel mulches the plants, keeping roots cool but not soggy, and it extends to the pathways for a unified surface.

Flowering bulbs like grape hyacinth (*Muscari armeniacum*) and daffodil (*Narcissus* 'Ice Wings' and 'Sundial', among others) join irises in coloring the slope blue and yellow in early spring. Then the orange cups of California poppy (*Eschscholzia californica*), rocket-shaped flowers of columbine (*Aquilegia vulgaris*), and clove-scented dianthus (*Dianthus* spp.) take over. By summer a carpet of pink creeping thyme (*Thymus praecox* ssp. *arcticus*) fills in among the stones, with the blond plumes of Mexican feathergrass (*Nassella tenuissima*) waving above. Tennessee coneflower (*Echinacea tennesseensis*), magenta winecup (*Callirhoe involucrata*), airy Russian sage (*Perovskia atriplicifolia*), and sunset-hued licorice mint (*Agastache rupestris*) offer hummingbirds and butterflies a tasty stop. Their blooms continue into early fall, with the addition of the lavender spikes of dwarf blazing star (*Liatris microcephala*) and the feathery plumes of 'Karl Foerster' feather reed grass (*Calamagrostis* x *acutiflora*) and ruby grass (*Melinis nerviglumis*). Set against an emerald border of trees, this kaleidoscope of color and fine-leaved texture resists wilting even in the heat of summer. As in all gravel gardens, a firm hand with weeding is necessary, since gravel is a perfect medium for self-sown seeds.

For anyone troubled by a dry slope where lawn shrivels each summer, this garden shows how beautiful a low-water gravel garden can be instead.

Opposite: Hardy ice plant (*Delosperma cooperi*) doesn't melt in summer's heat.

Below left: Bands of stone casually terrace the slope and create a path.

Below center: Tennessee coneflower (*Echinacea tennesseensis*) adds a rosy color in the summer.

Below right: Flowering perennials brighten a narrow gravel path.

bold foliage takes center stage

John Kuzma Garden, Portland, Oregon

Although the Pacific Northwest has a reputation for being rainy, its summers are generally sunny and dry. During those summer months without rain, lawns turn to straw and plants that thrive in moist soils suffer drought stress. While some people are content to let their lawns go dormant until fall rains return, and others water to keep lawns green, Portland resident John Kuzma decided to do away with his lawn altogether in favor of bold-foliage, mainly dry-loving plants from all over the world. His large, half-acre lot, formerly carpeted with lawn, offered no privacy from neighboring two-story houses and uninteresting views from inside his own home. Regrading solved both issues and created fast-draining berms that allow dry-adapted plants to thrive in Portland's cool, wet winters.

This page: A focal-point water feature can be a potent symbol in a low-water garden.

Opposite left: Drought-tolerant kangaroo paws (*Anigozanthos* spp.) bloom in bermed beds.

Opposite right: Where winding gravel paths meet up in the center of the garden, a large unplanted pot marks the crossroads.

Designed by Sean Hogan of Cistus, the now-lawnless back garden offers a split-level experience. Just off the patio, an expansive, basalt-gravel terrace extends the home's entertaining space and leads the eye to a dramatic focal-point view: a trough-style fountain backed by a long raised bed of textural grasses, palms, yucca, kangaroo paws, and other plants with bold form and striking leaf texture and color. The large gravel terrace needs no watering, of course, and allows rainwater to soak into the ground rather than running off into the street. A few feet above it, and accessed via steps to the left and right of the trough fountain, the main garden tantalizes with dramatic evergreen plants like agave, prickly pear, and yucca intermingled with silver acacia, bronze rushes, and sunset-hued flowering perennials. Atop a broad berm that parallels the house, dense plantings screen the home from view of the neighbors, and plants are elevated for eye-level appreciation.

Bold and spiky plants need space in order to be garden- and gardener-friendly. Hogan laid basalt gravel throughout the garden for a continuous surface that keeps roots cool in the garden beds and provides broad, winding paths—a continuation of the gravel terrace below. Where paths converge from different areas of the garden, the gravel paving widens into a sort of courtyard, which Kuzma anchors with a solitary, unplanted orange pot—an irresistible focal point that draws you into the garden.

One side of the garden is more lushly planted, with magnolias and leafy shrubs in berms mulched with shredded wood instead of gravel. A blue pot attracts the eye at the end of a narrow path in this softer section of the garden. Unplanted pots make beautiful focal points and require no water to maintain, unlike planted pots, which often need watering daily or even twice a day in hot weather. Drainage holes keep water from collecting—and mosquitoes from breeding—when it rains.

Left: A diagonal path leads the eye to a focal-point pot.

Right: Planted high on berms, bold-foliage plants help screen neighboring houses.

Native palo blanco trees (*Acacia willardiana*) and desert marigold (*Baileya multiradiata*) grow in a terraced garden with a dry stream at the bottom.

evoking water in a dry garden

Scottsdale Xeriscape Demonstration Garden,
Scottsdale, Arizona

"The frog does not drink up the pond in which he lives." These words, inscribed on the rim of a brimming water feature in the Xeriscape Demonstration Garden in Scottsdale, Arizona, remind us of what's at stake when we overconsume our water supply. The garden itself is an eloquent reminder that we don't have to. Built atop a buried reservoir of municipal drinking water, this public garden models sustainable water use and shows just how beautiful a low-water garden can be.

Anchoring the north entrance, the brimming vessel of water is a symbol of abundance in the Moorish garden tradition—an oasis in an arid climate. Birds, insects, and other wildlife come here to drink, and it nourishes the human visitor's spirit too, especially during the heat of summer. Water—its scarcity and the various methods of collecting it during the rainy monsoon season—drives the entire garden's design.

the water-saving garden

Throughout much of the garden, gabion walls—wire cages filled with rocks—are used to terrace the soil, creating flat beds for planting. When the rains come, the terraces shed less water than a slope would, and the walls further slow its passage across the property. Water that would otherwise be lost is now held in place, allowing a slow soak into parched soil.

Thoughtful plant selection takes advantage of soil and rain conditions. At higher points in the garden, where soil stays dry, native ocotillo (*Fouquieria splendens*), golden barrel cactus (*Echinocactus grusonii*), and spring-blooming desert marigold (*Baileya multiradiata*) thrive in full sun with little water.

At a low point, a sunken amphitheater outlined by spiraling low walls, which functions as one of the garden's outdoor classrooms, is designed to collect runoff during rainstorms. A bosque of honey mesquite (*Prosopis glandulosa*) trees, which tolerate seasonal flooding, offers filtered shade, making this a desert-style rain garden.

Opposite: Native ocotillo (*Fouquieria splendens*) and golden barrel cactus (*Echinocactus grusonii*) add architectural structure to the garden.

Above left: Broadly curving gabion walls terrace a slope to prevent runoff.

Above right: Stone steps and terracing evoke a cascading waterfall.

An amphitheater doubles as a desert-style rain garden.

The most spectacular feature of the garden is an environmental artwork by Lorna Jordan called *Terraced Cascade*—a melding of art, native plants, stonework, and water harvesting that represents both the human spine and a cascading waterfall (see photo on page 27). It's a physical imagining of our own place within the natural landscape, as well as our mutual dependence on water. Rib-like walls constructed of ledge stone, accented by bands of river rock, terrace the garden and create level beds for ghostly palo blanco trees (*Acacia willardiana*) and silvery desert marigold (*Baileya multiradiata*). Threading through the center, a stone stair seems to splash its way downhill from the rim to the water-collecting basin at the bottom. This magical waterway is evoked solely through stone!

When it rains, water flows down the cascading steps and into a dry stream spanned by two steel bridges (see photo on page 25). French drains at the bottom of the basin direct overflow to a nearby lake, from which water is drawn at dry times of the year to irrigate the garden.

part two

make your garden
a WATER SAVER,
not a WATER GUZZLER

hold that liquid gold

Wherever you live, whether your climate is arid or
rainy or somewhere in-between, designing your garden
to keep rainwater from leaving your property makes
good sense environmentally and financially.

Rainwater is liquid money. After all, if it rains enough, you don't have to
water your garden. And if you have rainwater stored up, you can use it
to water during a dry spell while keeping the city water turned off. Has
your water rate gone up in recent years? In drought-stricken states with
mandatory watering restrictions, water utilities may raise their rates because
their earnings plummet when people reduce their water usage. In such
cases you may find you're paying more to use less water. Saving rainwater
can make up the difference for your garden.

From a gardening perspective, plants prefer rainwater to treated tap water,
which can cause harmful mineral buildup in the soil. And from a broader
environmental viewpoint, holding rainwater on your property helps keep
pollutants out of your water supply. How? Our yards are designed to shed
water. When a house is built, the lot is graded so that water flows away from
the foundation and out to the street. From a home-building perspective, this
makes good sense. Water must be kept out of crawlspaces and basements to
prevent mildew, mold, and damage to the foundation. When grading is done
improperly, basements may flood or water may pool in the yard every time

Storing rainwater in
a large tank provides
a free source of water
for your garden.

Left: Even a brief rain will quickly fill a rain barrel.

Center: A decorative rain chain directs water from the eave into a barrel.

Right: Downspouts can be angled directly into a rain barrel.

it rains, creating swampy conditions. The usual solution involves rerouting water away from the house via French drains, gutters, and downspouts, funneling runoff through buried pipes out to the street.

For dry-climate gardeners, that's money down the drain. But even for those in rainier parts of the country, this isn't a good thing because of how runoff impacts drinking-water supplies. Would you willingly drink water from the gutter? Consider where that puddle comes from. Rainwater washing into the gutter carries motor oil, antifreeze, cigarette butts, and other pollutants from the road. When water runs off the lawn, whether through irrigation or a rainstorm, it picks up fertilizers, pesticides, and animal waste. This toxic soup pours through storm drains and into local creeks. The creeks feed the rivers and lakes that serve as sources of drinking water for many of us—we drink from the gutter without even realizing it.

Our water utilities treat and filter this water so that we can drink it without getting sick. But it would be better to strip away many of these impurities before they even reach our water supplies. Plants can do this for us! Living filters, plants cleanse pollutants out of water as it soaks through the soil and moves through their roots. If you can trap rainwater on your property and either store it for future use or give it time to soak into the soil (away from your foundation), you can directly impact the purity of your water supply. On a larger scale, developers can design streets so that runoff from the road flows into curbside rain gardens for filtering rather than straight into storm drains—a growing practice that's particularly important in highly paved urban areas.

The traditional landscaping goal of moving water swiftly away from the house and into storm drains is as outdated as a home garden that requires daily watering and a staff of gardeners. It's not an environmentally smart choice, and it's costly in terms of potential savings lost. Instead, a water-saving garden treats water as a bankable resource, storing it up for a dry (not rainy) day or slowing it down to give it time to filter into the soil. Let's take a look at various ways of capturing, storing, and recycling water in the garden.

rain barrels and cisterns

Nothing makes a dry-climate gardener happier than the sound of rain drumming on the roof and the sight of a full-to-the-brim rain barrel. Rainwater collection isn't just for water-challenged gardeners, however. People the world over have long used tanks, buckets, barrels, and stone cisterns to collect and store rainwater, and it's as effective and easy to set up today as it's ever been.

How easy? Well, setting a watertight container under your eave and waiting for rain to fill it up is pretty easy. But you can collect rainwater much more efficiently by installing gutters on your roof and placing rain barrels under your downspouts. If you already have gutters, lucky you! Just use a hacksaw to shorten an existing downspout, add a short, curved elbow section to the end of the downspout to direct water flow away from the house, and position your rain barrel underneath it. For a more decorative look, hang a rain chain in place of the downspout and enjoy the sight and musical sound of water filling the tank.

A 1,000-gallon cistern holds water for a vegetable garden.

Two large cisterns collect water from the roof for use in this garden.

Aside from being watertight, rain barrels and cisterns should be opaque in order to keep out sunlight, which stimulates the growth of algae. In other words, don't use translucent plastic containers, or you'll soon have water resembling pea soup. Containers should also be topped with a fine-screened lid to keep mosquitoes from breeding inside and to keep out rodents, birds, and other creatures. Consider elevating your barrel on concrete blocks or a wooden platform to improve water flow, which depends on gravity. For safety's sake, however, be sure the platform is level, stable, and strong enough to support the considerable weight of a full barrel, and if young children are present, securely attach the rain barrel to the house and secure the lid. Water is very heavy, and if a tank filled with water were to topple over on someone, it could cause serious harm. If you have young children or grandchildren, or if your rain barrel is located in an unfenced yard accessible to neighborhood kids, choose one that a child cannot climb or fall into. Such designs have narrow mouths, safety grids, or lockable lids. If you opt to use a recycled drum or other open-top container, you'll need to securely attach a screened lid with sturdy cross supports. Water is always a temptation for kids, so better to be extra safe than sorry.

Homeowner Karen Lantz checks the water level in her 1,400-gallon underground cistern.

While gravity flow is sufficient to fill a watering can or run a steady stream from a hose, if you wish to run a hose-end sprinkler with rainwater you'll need a larger cistern that can hold more water and a pump to create sufficient water pressure. Because roofs accumulate valve-clogging debris between rains— bird droppings, leaves and twigs, asphalt-shingle granules—large cisterns should be installed with a diverter pipe that collects the first flush of water off the roof, usually about 10 gallons, and that has a clean-out valve for easy disposal of soggy debris. If you have plenty of space, you can hook up multiple tanks in a row and connect them so that when the first tank is full, water is diverted to the second tank, and so on. On the other hand, if your lot is small

A 10,000-gallon cistern is partially hidden below a retaining wall.

or you have other space limitations, consider putting a cistern and pump underground. Burying a big tank is more expensive than setting it next to the house, not to mention disruptive to an established garden, so it's best considered during a new home's construction or during an extensive remodel, when things are already torn up.

What size rain barrel or cistern you choose will depend on a number of things: how much water you'd like to save, your budget, available space, and, not least, any relevant homeowners' association rules or state laws. (Colorado, for instance, does not allow rainwater collection by homeowners served by water utilities; only those who rely on well water and meet certain other conditions may collect what falls freely from the sky.) If you are determined to capture as much water as possible, you'll need to do a little math in order to calculate how much water your roof sheds in an average year. The rule of thumb is: 1 inch of rain falling on a 1,000-square-foot roof yields 600 gallons. Irregularly shaped roofs can make square footage calculations a bit tricky, and there's usually some loss of water between rain hitting the roof and its deposit into a rain barrel, but at least this formula

gives you an idea. If your region gets an annual average of, say, 14 inches of rain, like Los Angeles, that comes to about 8,400 gallons for the year off a 1,000-square-foot roof. In Dallas, which gets about 37 inches per year, that same roof yields 22,200 gallons. Obviously, you'll want to choose your cistern capacity accordingly. There's no need to splurge on a 10,000-gallon tank when a year's worth of rain can't fill it. And keep in mind that you'll be using collected water during dry times, so you likely won't be storing an entire year's worth of rainfall at any time.

Small- to medium-sized rain barrels can be purchased from garden centers, online gardening catalogs, home-improvement stores, and, in some cities, municipal conservation programs. Homemade rain collectors like wooden barrels and metal drums also work, although you should avoid any used container that may have held hazardous chemicals. Large tanks and cisterns (500-gallon to 20,000-gallon capacity) are generally sold at businesses that specialize in rainwater collection, and you'll likely need their expertise and help in setting up a cistern of this size. Whatever size you choose, keep in mind that rain barrels are the opposite of Mary Poppins's magical

Lightweight rain barrels that resemble terracotta urns blend gracefully into most gardens.

carpetbag: they fill up much faster than you might expect. Even a light rain can quickly top off a small cistern. To maximize collection and gain enough capacity to last you through dry spells, go with the biggest size you can afford, that fits into your garden, and that can hold your region's annual rainfall. Once you start hoarding free water, you'll wish you could save even more. But if you're limited to a small rain barrel, don't despair; you'll still find it useful. While a small barrel can't hold enough to irrigate your entire garden, it can be used to water potted plants on the patio, top off a fishpond, or run a slow drip on a thirsty tree. In other words, a rain barrel of any size is good to have.

Keep in mind that your rain barrel or cistern will have an overflow valve that releases surplus water when the tank is full. Small- to medium-sized rain barrels can fill to overflowing quickly, so when placing your barrel, give thought to where the overflow will go. Point the overflow valve away from your house and, ideally, into a dry stream that directs the runoff away from the foundation and into a rain garden filled with plants that can absorb the extra water. Read on for more information about rain gardens.

A safety note: For the purposes of this book, rainwater collection is assumed to be for watering plants, not for drinking, showering, or other household use. The latter may be subject to city code and necessitates precautions to ensure safety, since water collected off roofs picks up natural and chemical contaminants. While plants are excellent filters, people are not.

rain gardens

Rain barrels and cisterns can collect some rainwater that falls on your property, but they can hardly catch all of it. Aside from the overflow from the roof, there's runoff from hard surfaces like driveways and patios and, perhaps surprisingly, even from organic surfaces like sloping lawns. One way to capture this overflow is with a rain garden. In drier regions, a rain garden is an effective way to sop up all the rainwater that falls on your property in order to keep it in your garden. In wetter regions, rain gardens are increasingly popular as cities encourage their use to help

Left: A newly planted rain garden with a water-absorbing layer of mulch.

Right: Overflow from a large cistern is directed into a nearby rain garden.

keep waterways clean. As mentioned earlier, water flowing off a driveway picks up motor oil; from a lawn it may pick up fertilizers, pesticides, and animal waste. All of this runs into the gutter, joining runoff from other yards along the street, and flows into storm drains and then into our creeks, rivers, lakes, and bays.

A rain garden can stop the cycle of water loss and waterway pollution on a yard-by-yard basis. Essentially a bowl-like depression planted with plants that don't mind occasional flooding, a well-positioned rain garden collects runoff from downspouts, the driveway, and any other water-shedding surface. Designed to hold water for no more than 24 hours, a rain garden gives the soil time to absorb runoff while its plants do the dirty work of filtering out pollutants. Scrubbed clean, the water works its way deeper into the earth, recharging groundwater and aquifers. Planted appropriately, a rain garden can be a lovely feature in your garden as well as a hardworking one and will look good in the front or back yard. To top it off, birds, butterflies, and other beneficial creatures enjoy rain gardens too, so by making one, you're providing valuable habitat, and you get to enjoy their visits.

Making a rain garden is pretty simple. Instead of mounding good soil as you might do when creating a traditional garden bed, you dig out soil to make a rain garden. Choose a spot at least 10 feet away from your house so as not to invite water into the foundation or basement, and 50 feet from the septic system, if you have one. An already sunken part of your yard that tends to pond after a rain might seem like the perfect spot, but it's really not. Ponding indicates that water is not being absorbed into the soil as quickly as needed, and standing water also breeds mosquitoes. Instead, choose a higher, better-draining spot that will intercept runoff from downspouts, the driveway, or the lawn. Drainage is the key to success; otherwise you're creating a pond or a marsh. A rain garden should drain within 24 hours in order to effectively filter water through plant roots and into the soil and to prevent mosquitoes from breeding. Some types of soil have so much clay or underlying bedrock that water cannot drain quickly and won't be appropriate for a rain garden. How do you know if a rain garden will work for you? Before you start excavating, do a simple drainage test: dig a hole about 12 inches deep, fill it halfway with water, and see how long it takes for the water to be absorbed into the soil. If it drains within 24 hours, you're in business. If it takes longer, your soil may not be suitable for a rain garden, although sometimes amending the soil with several inches of compost and small pea gravel can help.

Rain gardens of nearly any size help filter runoff, so you really can't go wrong, even with a small one. But the bigger it is, the more rainwater you can hold on your property and keep out of the storm drains. It may be most effective to build two—one for the front yard and one for the back—with drainage pipes funneling water from downspouts into the rain gardens. Before you dig, call your local utilities (some cities offer a "call before you dig" phone number) to make sure a gas, electric, or water line doesn't run through the chosen location; if it does, shift your planned rain garden to a

Above: Lawn runoff flows into a rain garden planted with water-loving iris. A drainage pipe under the gravel walk extends the rain garden to each side of the path.

Left: A lush rain garden absorbs runoff from paving.

Large rain gardens are designed to handle runoff in commercial developments.

different part of your yard. Also, avoid siting your new rain garden under the canopy of an existing tree, as excavation will damage feeder roots, and periodic flooding may drown the tree.

Residential rain gardens can be dug by hand or by a small backhoe, and generally 4 to 8 inches is deep enough to hold runoff; the shallower your rain garden, the larger it should be in order to hold a similar capacity. However, you need to excavate 4 or 5 inches deeper than your final expected depth in order to leave room for added compost and mulch. Use some of the excavated topsoil to build up the downhill edge of your rain garden, keeping the rim level all the way around and enabling it to hold water on a gentle slope. Excess soil can be used to create water-directing berms that funnel water into the rain garden or to build up raised beds elsewhere on your property. Oval and kidney-shaped rain gardens look most natural in the landscape, but contemporary, straight-edged designs, especially when bordered by stone or concrete, work well in urban locations or in contemporary gardens.

Once you've dug out the rain garden, add 3 to 4 inches of compost to loosen the soil and prepare it for planting. Choose a mix of grasses, perennials, and shrubs that can handle occasional periods of standing water. Unless it rains all the time where you live, avoid bog plants, which won't appreciate going dry between rains. Rather, deep-rooted grasses and adaptable native perennials and shrubs will be your best choices. If you're not sure what plants to choose, check with your local extension office or trusted local nursery for recommendations. Many cities that encourage citizens to install rain gardens offer detailed how-to guides and plant lists appropriate to the local climate, which you can find online.

Don't try to establish a rain garden from seed, as influxes of water will likely wash out the seed or drown tiny seedlings. Instead, buy 1-gallon or larger plants from your local nursery, or use generous divisions of plants like daylilies and grasses from other parts of your garden. Plants native to your region and naturally found atop the banks of streams and in meadows and prairies can be excellent choices because they've evolved to withstand dry periods interrupted by seasonal flooding. While they're getting established, you'll need to water regularly between rains to ensure good root growth. Once your rain garden is established, it shouldn't need much supplemental watering—maybe only during excessively dry periods. After planting, mulch the garden with 1 to 2 inches of nonfloating wood mulch. Shredded hardwood mulch is a good choice; avoid bark mulch, which washes away in rain like so many toy boats. Be sure to weed regularly in the first couple of years to keep your rain garden tidy and prevent its being overrun with coarse, unattractive weeds from seeds that wash in. Over time, as your chosen plants develop deep and spreading roots and their leaves crowd together to shade the soil, weeds will have stiff competition and become less of a concern.

curb-cut gardens

Excitingly, rain gardens can also be designed in reverse to capture water from the street. Cities like Portland, Oregon, are leading the way in reducing stormwater runoff by integrating rain gardens into city streets, turning on its head the old model of shunting water from pavement and roads into storm drains. In the green-street model, water running in the gutter is captured via curb cuts that allow it to flow into small, sunken rain gardens between the street and sidewalk. Planted with grasses and other perennials,

Above: Curb cuts allow runoff from a parking lot to enter a water-cleansing bioswale garden.

Left: A bioswale garden in the High Point neighborhood in West Seattle, Washington, collects street runoff.

Right: In Portland, Oregon, curbing along a residential street is bumped out into the roadway so that a curb cut can capture runoff. A bioswale garden planted in the bump-out cleans contaminants and adds natural beauty.

the gardens filter out pollutants and green up public spaces. Where once a sea of concrete and asphalt shed water and added to the urban heat island effect, green-street rain gardens add beauty to city streets, create urban wildlife habitat, help replenish groundwater, and cool the air temperature in summer.

Stormwater harvesting can be implemented on a home-by-home basis through curb cuts, if your city allows. Curb cuts are simply the removal of a small section of curbing, usually no more than 2 feet in length, between your yard and the street in order to let water flow into your yard when it rains. They work best when located near a stormwater drain so that water can be intercepted before carrying road pollutants into local creeks. And of course the soil level at the curb cut must be slightly lower than the gutter in order to capture water flowing downhill, although all that this requires is excavation of a shallow basin, as with any rain garden. Tucson, Arizona, resident and rainwater activist Brad Lancaster convinced his city to make curb cutting legal by showing how curb cuts divert thousands of gallons of stormwater runoff into a shallow basin along the frontage of his property, which he's planted with native and desert-adapted trees, shrubs, and perennials that thrive on the extra water. With wise plant choices, his rain garden—and others like it—needs no supplemental irrigation of pumped-in water from the city. Instead it's transformed his property into an oasis of vegetation that provides wildlife habitat and cooling shade, even as it purifies runoff and saves the city money. As with traditional rain gardens, curb-cut gardens work equally well in dry and wet climates. They make the most of natural rainfall in dry climates, and in wetter regions, they provide an easy way for individuals to make a difference in reducing water pollution.

Before making a curb cut, check your city's codes to see if it's legal. Some communities require residents to apply for a permit and have a licensed professional perform the work, while others allow residents to do it themselves. Some cities don't allow it at all. If that's the case in your city, you might wish to follow Brad Lancaster's example and lobby for legalization.

earth-sculpting: berms, microbasins, swales, and terraces

House lots are designed to shed water away from the foundation. Traditionally they're considered well graded if they keep runoff moving all the way out to the street, sending rainwater gushing into stormwater drains, along with hitchhiking pollutants, and out to local waterways. Then, when the rains stop and the soil dries out, the sprinklers switch on to spray costly city-treated, pumped-in water over the lawn and garden. It's clear that this water cycle makes little sense.

Grading, or sculpting the soil on your property, can help you hold the water that falls on your lot, which not only saves you money on your water bill but also benefits the environment by reducing erosion, keeping soil moist and better able to absorb summer heat, giving trees and other plants a deep drink every time it rains, replenishing groundwater and aquifers, and keeping pollutants picked up by runoff out of the water supply. For dry-climate gardeners, it's an excellent way to harvest rainwater that can keep plants alive. Whether it involves mounding soil into berms, carving it into swales, or flattening it into terraces, grading is a tool that every homeowner can use to make his or her garden a water saver.

BERMING AND MICROBASINS

There are various ways of using mounded soil to capture rainwater, and the slope of your property—or your neighbor's property—will determine the best choice for your situation. For nearly level or shallow slopes, berming is a good choice. Berming soil to create water-collecting basins is an ancient technique, used two thousand years ago by farmers in the Middle East. It's just as effective today. Essentially a mini-dam, bermed soil holds runoff behind it in what's known as a microbasin, giving it time to percolate into the soil. A series of microbasins arrayed on a gentle slope can catch and hold even more runoff. As water pools behind and then overruns one berm, it moves downhill to the next one in its path and pools behind that one, and so on. Slowed from an erosive rush to a leisurely amble, runoff is captured and contained in the soil.

To create a microbasin, mound soil in broad arcs, like outstretched arms facing upslope to embrace the runoff, spaced like ripples widening outward from the source of runoff—typically the roof or driveway. Landscape architect Christine Ten Eyck's personal garden in Austin, Texas (see page 17), is an excellent example of how microbasins can slow runoff and give it time to soak into the soil. When Ten Eyck removed a large lawn from her front yard, which sloped toward the street and shed an enormous amount of water during heavy rainstorms, she constructed wide, curving check dams with rocks found on her property, creating microbasins to collect runoff. Her goal was to hold every bit of water falling on her property, and microbasins proved an effective tool for slowing water and giving it time to infiltrate the soil. Native shrubs, small trees, perennials, and grasses thrive in the microbasins, where they enjoy a long, slow drink every time it rains.

Microbasins should not be constructed in the path of a drainage channel where water flows swiftly during a rain, nor too close to the foundation of your home. You still want water to move away from your home's foundation, so think of your water-shedding roof or driveway as a rock dropped in a pond, with microbasins as ripples at least 10 feet away and spreading

A low check dam slows and holds water behind it.

outward and downhill. (You can also berm soil to catch water uphill from your home, but again, this method is best suited to nearly flat, not steeply sloping, lots.) Excavate a shallow basin and use the dug-out soil to build up a crescent-shaped berm on the downhill side of the basin. Compact the berm by stomping all over it and tamping the soil in place, and consider lining it with rocks so that the berm doesn't wash away when runoff pools behind it. The basin itself, however, should not be tamped down, as loose, fluffy soil absorbs water better than compacted soil and better supports plant life, holds soil in place, and filters runoff. Piled rocks in the form of gabion walls (rocks encased in wire for stability) or simple check dams can be used instead of bermed soil, as Ten Eyck did, if you have plenty of rocks on hand. Microbasins should not be deep; you're not trying to create a pond but rather a shallow depression in which water can collect. A basin depth that is 12 to 18 inches lower than the bermed edge should be sufficient. Any overflow can be collected in lower microbasins "rippling" outward. As with rain gardens, water should soak into the soil within 24 hours in order to prevent mosquitoes from breeding, so check your soil's permeability before starting construction.

Planting your microbasins is important for erosion control and for filtering runoff, plus it helps them blend into the overall design of your garden. The roots of plants will spread into the berms and stabilize them, and low-growing stems and branches help slow water even further. The plants

Below left: In a desert garden, berms can be used to direct precious rainwater to plants.

Below right: Soil is bermed in an arc on the downhill side of this water-wise garden to create a water-holding microbasin.

the water-saving garden

you choose must be able to tolerate occasional periods of extra water, so don't plant your most dry-loving plants in the basin. Prairie grasses, sedges, and streamside or dry-wash perennials are good choices. Check with your local extension office, a good local nursery, or online for rain-garden plants appropriate to your region, or simply experiment with divisions from your existing garden or friends' gardens to see what thrives.

Above left: A broad, curving swale is lushly planted.

Above right: On a smaller scale, a narrow swale running alongside a driveway collects water that flows in from uphill.

SWALES

Creating a swale is the opposite of making a berm: instead of being mounded, soil is excavated to create a shallow gully, usually only 6 to 12 inches deep. Laid lengthwise along a gentle slope, a swale collects runoff flowing downhill and holds it until it overflows. While the water is pooling in the swale, some of it soaks into the ground. The overflow spills out and continues downhill to the next swale and so on. The soaking-and-spillover process slows down the water significantly and gives it time to replenish the soil.

A swale can also be laid out like a stream, with natural-looking broad curves, at the lower end of a gentle slope in order to collect runoff that is then funneled to a rain garden. In this case, the swale isn't slowing a downhill flow of water so much as gathering it and moving it to where it can be absorbed.

Country roads as well as some neighborhood streets in cities like Houston incorporate swales as drainage ditches alongside the road. Such grassy, often weedy, ditches have given swales a bad rap, but they can be so much more. Lazily curved and naturalistically planted with reeds, grasses, or other plants that enjoy occasional extra water, a swale can be an attractive feature in a garden. Essentially a wet-weather stream, a swale offers habitat for wildlife and natural beauty, even as it moves water where you want it to go. Similar in purpose, a dry stream is a swale dressed up with rocks (see page 189).

TERRACES

If your property sits on a steep slope, you likely have erosion problems in addition to dry soil that can't hold water long enough for it to soak in. Shallow swales and microbasins aren't suitable for slowing and holding large volumes of runoff on a hillside. However, you can terrace your slope for the same result. Happily, terraces also create useable space on a steep slope, giving you room for a seating area or play space and a garden where it may previously have been difficult even to walk.

Terraces are flat areas carved into a hillside, like steps a giant might use to walk uphill. The flattened ground gives rainwater and runoff time to soak in rather than coursing straight downhill. Planted with deep-rooted shrubs, grasses, and perennials and mulched to cover bare soil, terraces soak up water like sponges and prevent erosion; the resulting garden gives usable outdoor space for entertaining, growing edibles or favorite ornamentals, and a play area for kids and pets. Terracing can be as straightforward as making two level spaces out of a short slope, as in my current garden, where I terraced a hard-to-mow, hard-to-walk-on, water-shedding natural berm to make plantable garden space and a water-permeable path (see photos on page 52). On the other hand, it may be as complex as taming a steep cliff with multiple retaining walls at various levels. If the terraced garden rises above the elevation of the house, it can also provide a beautiful view from inside the home—so much better than an eroded, weedy slope.

BEFORE

AFTER

While it's not easy work, you can terrace a slope yourself if you keep the rise between "steps"—that is, the retaining walls—no higher than 2 feet (generally accepted as the maximum recommended height for DIYers to attempt) and set back each upper wall a distance that's twice the height of the wall below it. Soil is very heavy, and when saturated after a rain, it puts a tremendous amount of pressure on a retaining wall. The pressure can cause a dangerous failure of a poorly constructed retaining wall, leading to collapse and soil movement. If any of your terrace walls needs to be more than 2 feet tall due to a steep slope or space constraints, enlist a skilled contractor to build them; a drainage engineer may also be necessary if you're terracing above your house or neighboring houses, where runoff management is essential to prevent flooding or foundation damage.

For more basic projects that you can attempt yourself, first call your local utilities or your city's "call before you dig" hotline to locate any buried lines or pipes in the area where you'll be terracing. If lines are present, you won't be able to excavate very deeply and will probably need to consider alternative methods of stabilizing your slope, like planting dense groundcovers to reduce erosion and installing a French drain (a slightly sloped, gravel-filled trench, sometimes laid with perforated pipe, which

Before: A steep slope makes mowing and watering difficult.

After: Terracing walls create water-absorbing planting beds.

BEFORE

AFTER

Before: A grassy slope shed water when it rained, and the lawn became drought stressed.

After: A stacked-stone retaining wall created a level space for planting and carved out room below for a gravel path.

collects and diverts water) at the base of the hill. Next, decide what you want your retaining walls to be made of. Common choices include stone (stacked flagstone or cut stone for low walls; cut stone blocks for higher walls), pre-formed cement blocks that lock together and are meant to resemble stone (easy to work with and less expensive but lacking natural stone's good looks), urbanite (slabs of broken concrete from an old sidewalk, patio, or driveway, an ecologically friendly choice that recycles material otherwise destined for the landfill), concrete blocks (for a plain, modern look, although they can be painted or stuccoed), and pressure-treated timbers (which contain chemical preservatives not recommended for frequent human contact or for use near edibles). Railroad ties are not recommended because they contain creosote, a known carcinogen, nor is untreated wood, which quickly rots.

Start by excavating a level space at the bottom of the slope; this will be your first terrace. Once you've leveled your lowest terrace, dig a flat-bottomed trench along the slope and running the length of the terrace and curve it into the hillside at each end; this is where you'll build a retaining wall to support the soil above. The depth of the trench depends on how high the retaining wall will be, but generally it should be deep enough to hide and secure the bottom course of your wall-building material plus an additional 4 to 6 inches of compacted gravel or road base. If you're using stone blocks that are 8 inches tall, for example, your trench should be at least 12 inches deep. Spread a 4- to 6-inch layer of sharp, angular gravel (not rounded pea gravel) or road base in the trench and compact it firmly with a hand tamper or a mechanical compactor. Make sure the compacted base is level, not sloping, by laying a straight piece of lumber in the trench and reading a hand level placed on top. A compacted, level base is a key component of a stable wall.

Now you can begin building your retaining wall on the compacted base. Remember to keep your wall under 2 feet high for safety reasons; otherwise hire a professional. As you build, step back each course (or layer) of your building material—that is, lay each subsequent course a little closer to the slope. This strengthens the wall against the force of soil pushing against it. Also, stagger the building material units across joint lines, rather than stacking them perfectly atop one another, for increased strength. When your wall reaches the desired height, start excavating into the slope above it to level out your next terrace, and so on.

When your terrace or terraces are complete, loosen the top couple of inches of soil, which were likely compacted during construction. Add a layer of compost to improve the health of the soil and its ability to soak up rain or runoff. Finally, plant your terraced garden. Whatever you choose, the plants will enjoy the extra water that the terraces are able to hold, and you'll gain a beautiful garden in the process.

greywater and air-conditioning condensate

We've explored ways of capturing rainwater and stormwater runoff, but there's another readily available source of water that could potentially supply much of your irrigation needs: greywater. It's the water that drains out of your shower, bathtub, bathroom sink, and washing machine. It's called "grey"—that is, slightly dirty—because it contains soap, detergent, and dirt, but your plants won't mind it. (Those using greywater should use nontoxic, low-sodium soaps and detergents to avoid harmful buildups in the soil, and avoid using bleach, which can kill plants.) Greywater does not typically

Shallow terraced beds turn a steep slope into a vertical garden.

include water from the kitchen sink or the dishwasher, which may contain grease and food particles that can clog pipes, attract rodents, and smell bad, nor does it include water flushed down the toilet or used to wash diapers, for obvious reasons of sanitation and public health.

According to the Environmental Protection Agency, the average American family of four uses about 170 gallons of indoor water per day that could safely be put to use in a greywater recycling system. One simple thing almost anyone can do to collect greywater is to put a bucket under the

THE LEGALITY OF GREYWATER SYSTEMS

Traditionally, state regulations governing residential plumbing have considered greywater to be the same as sewage from the toilet: wastewater to be disposed of. That's too bad. As fresh water becomes scarcer due to drought and population growth, and as treated water grows more expensive, it makes good sense to find ways of reusing water in the landscape that would otherwise be sent into the wastewater system. If you're interested in outfitting your home with a greywater system, first check your state's regulations. Greywater policies vary from state to state, and plumbing alterations are often banned for reasons pertaining to public health and safety. As public interest grows and water supplies dwindle, however, regulations may be loosened. If your state restricts greywater use, consider writing to your legislator to ask for a change, pointing out how it helps with water conservation and wastewater treatment costs—two issues of vital importance no matter where you live.

---

showerhead to fill while waiting for the water to heat up and while showering. That water can then be carried outdoors to use on the garden. But if you want to recycle all of your greywater, you need a system of plumbing pipes, filters, and valves to divert water from your wastewater line into your garden. Drought-prone countries like Australia are way ahead of the United States in encouraging residential use of greywater, but the United States is slowly catching up, especially in the desert Southwest. Tucson, Arizona, for example, now requires new homes to have greywater drains and outside hookups so that water from the washing machine, bathtub, and shower can be used in the landscape.

If your state allows greywater collection systems (see above), keep the following safety information in mind. Because of potential bacteria buildup, greywater should not be stored longer than 24 hours. It should be allowed to soak into the soil right away. Loosened soil and mulch around your plants will aid in its absorption. Again, be sure to use low-sodium and low-boron soaps and detergents—and don't use bleach—in your washing machine, tub, and shower so that your greywater will be safe for your plants. Also, greywater is best used on ornamental plants rather than edibles whose leaves or other edible parts might come in contact with bacteria-laden water. Go ahead and water fruit and nut trees with greywater. However, avoid using it on root vegetables or low-growing plants like lettuces since the edible parts will come in contact with the greywater.

For a full greywater system that taps into shower and bathroom sink water, hire a plumber who has greywater experience to install the proper lines and valves. This will be affordable only where the existing plumbing is accessible, as in a pier-and-beam home or one with a basement—that is, not sealed in a slab foundation. Using greywater from the washing machine, however, is much easier and less costly to set up and requires no plumbing alterations. A so-called laundry-to-landscape system, in which laundry water is captured from the discharge hose and redirected via 1-inch irrigation pipes into the landscape, can be installed by a DIYer for just a few hundred dollars. Attaching a diverter valve to the washer's discharge hose allows you to choose whether to send water into the garden or into the sewer line (if you've run a load with bleach, for example, or if the ground is already saturated and can't absorb more). Look for complete instructions online at greywateraction.org and harvestingrainwater.com.

It's easy to collect air-conditioning condensate.

Another source of free water that comes out of your house is air-conditioning system condensate. An air conditioner works by pulling humidity out of your home, and as the moisture condenses on the evaporator coil, it drains out of the unit. In hot climates, A/C units produce a surprising amount of condensate each day—as much as 2 gallons from a window unit and between 5 and 20 gallons from a whole-house unit, depending on the humidity level of your climate. To take advantage of this free, pure water in the garden, you can plant moisture-loving plants around your A/C unit. If your unit is located above the level of your garden, even if the slope is slight, you can excavate a swale or dry stream that starts at the A/C drip line and runs to a rain garden. Or simply route the condensate via tube extensions downhill, using gravity to move the flow of condensate toward plants that appreciate extra water in summer. Easiest of all, you can dig a bucket-sized hole beneath your A/C drip line and let the condensate fill a bucket, or place a bucket beneath a window unit's drainage tube. (For safety around small children, don't use open buckets, into which a curious toddler could topple and drown.) Dumping the water once a day on a thirsty plant will keep mosquitoes from breeding in the bucket.

Terracing and dry-loving plants help transform a steep slope into a beautiful garden.

think saltines:
choose permeable paving

Paving is an unsung hero of our gardens. Often seen merely as a utilitarian material that keeps our feet dry, makes a level and comfortable surface for walking or seating, and keeps our cars out of the mud, paving is, above all, practical and hard-working. Thoughtfully designed and installed with skilled craftsmanship, it can also be beautiful. But whether humble or artful, paving can do even more for us: it can be an essential part of a water-saving garden.

Common paving materials like concrete, asphalt, and mortared stone deflect water like an umbrella. Unable to soak in, water flows off on a downhill path, which is typically graded by the builder to send runoff racing into the gutter. There it becomes a stormwater and waterway pollution problem to be dealt with—an expense that your city passes on to you in your water bill—rather than an asset to the garden if held on-site. This is free rainwater that we should be holding until the soil can absorb it and plants filter it. Why pay double, first in stormwater costs and then again to irrigate because the soil is dry? The key is to make your paving—driveway, walkways, patios—not a solid, water-shedding surface but porous, with entry points for water to soak into the soil (imagine a saltine cracker pocked with holes). The gaps for water absorption may be quite large if you use gravel or flagstones as paving,

A low stone retaining wall edges this arbor-shaded gravel patio.

or they may be small if you use unmortared brick or permeable concrete pavers. But these and other porous paving options can make a big difference for your soil and your garden, not to mention the health of local waterways.

Of course, not everyone has the means or desire to replace existing, serviceable, impervious paving, and it may make more sense to focus on other methods of saving water in your garden. But if you're building a new home or driveway or redoing your landscaping, you have an opportunity to make smart, water-saving choices. Perhaps you can reduce the overall footprint of your paving or replace a circular driveway blanketing half the front yard in concrete with a narrower drive so as to reduce the paved surface. Or, radically, you might remove the driveway altogether and park on the street (if city codes or HOA rules allow, and if street parking is not so limited that you'd be searching for parking far from home), freeing up more room for gardening or patio living while increasing your property's water-absorbing capacity.

Remember, though, that paving is not *bad*. In fact, it's beneficial to garden enjoyment to have generous areas of paving that invite people into the garden. Well-designed paving—not an endless sea of concrete, mind you, but an attractive patio or path—can also function as negative space, just as a lawn does. Since a thirsty lawn is ill suited to dry regions like the U.S. Southwest, Mountain States, and High Plains, paved outdoor-living spaces can take up space that's often defaulted to lawn. When you're trying to use less water, that's a good way to go.

gravel

The simplest, least-expensive paving that lets water through is gravel. The crunch of gravel on paths and drives is pleasing to the ear and can even serve as a security alert. It's easy to spread and lasts a long time, with only occasional retopping needed. On the downside, gravel can require regular weeding, and if you live in a snowy climate, it's not easy to shovel or plow snow off it. On a driveway, it can become rutted or potholed, although concrete parking strips can be added to provide a firm driving surface;

Gravel makes an economical and visually pleasing choice for any style of garden.

Gravel laid in a geometric design suits a contemporary garden.

even with the addition of impervious concrete strips, such driveways are still able to absorb quite a lot of water. For a path or patio, gravel is an excellent choice that works well with all garden styles.

Because heavy runoff can float or erode gravel, save gravel paving for a level or slightly sloping surface. If you want to lay a gravel path on a steeper slope, first terrace the path to create level areas for laying gravel. Angular gravel works best on terraced paths because it knits together and doesn't travel as much as, say, pea gravel. In level areas of the garden, all types of gravel will work. Pea gravel, consisting of round pebbles that shift easily underfoot, can be a slog to walk on if spread too thickly and therefore should be installed in a thin layer over a compacted base of granite dust or decomposed granite. In the Southwest, decomposed granite, a fine-textured, pulverized gravel that compacts to a nearly solid surface, is itself a popular choice for paving. While less permeable than coarser gravels, it does still admit water during a rain, and its firm surface also allows wheelchair users and bike riders to traverse it with ease.

Laying a gravel path or patio is easy. Dig out sod and soil to a depth of about 4 inches. Skip the landscape fabric unless you have suckering tree roots, in which case a heavy-duty, contractor's grade weed block fabric may be useful in suppressing them. Generally, however, weed block fabric won't prevent weed seeds from blowing in and germinating in the top layer of your gravel, and it's a curse-inducing chore to pull weeds whose roots have become enmeshed in it. Also, never use plastic as a weed block. It does not allow rainwater to soak into the ground, which defeats the purpose of using a permeable paving material.

Blue slag glass edges a gravel path.

Next, install a durable edging material. Stone blocks, large river rocks, bricks, pavers, bender board, and flexible steel landscape edging are all good choices, but you can get creative if you like. I've seen bowling balls, half-buried wine bottles, and colorful slag glass used as gravel edging. Do avoid inexpensive plastic edging, however, which rarely holds up well and tends to pop out of the ground over time.

Finally, lay the gravel. The depth depends on the type of gravel you choose. Decomposed granite should be compacted to a depth of 4 inches using a vibrating plate compactor or, for smaller spaces, a hand-held tamper. It may save you money to use less-expensive granite dust for the bottom 2 inches, with decomposed granite compacted for the top layer, 2 inches deep. Crushed gravel, which contains angular, larger stones than decomposed granite, can be laid to a depth of 4 inches and compacted lightly. Pea gravel should be laid to a depth of no more than 2 inches over a compacted, 2-inch layer of decomposed granite or granite dust for stability.

grid systems with grass

For driveways and parking courts, if you prefer a greener solution— literally greener—consider a concrete or heavy-duty plastic grid system with cells that support grass or a grassy groundcover like dwarf mondo grass (*Ophiopogon japonicus* 'Nanus'). It's an effective, attractive choice for driveways in temperate climates with adequate rainfall to keep the grass plugs alive on an exposed, heat-reflecting surface. (In hot or arid climates, fill the cells with gravel instead of grass. After all, it would defeat the purpose if you had to water your driveway.) The grid protects the grass, even from the weight of cars. Be aware, however, that if you park your car on it for days at a time, the grass may die from lack of sunlight.

Installation is a professional job. It requires removal of topsoil and compacting a layer of free-draining gravel that allows water to pass through. After installation, the cells are filled with a loamy soil mix, and grass is seeded or plugged into the holes. While the material cost is similar to that of a conventional concrete driveway, the installation cost tends to be higher, and you may find a shortage of experienced installers in your area.

unmortared stone, urbanite, bricks, and pavers

Flagstone is a classic choice for patios and paths, and if you choose a locally quarried stone, it gives your garden a sense of place, plus you'll pay less than you would for stone trucked in from far away. Thrifty, recycling-minded gardeners can use urbanite to the same effect. Urbanite is broken concrete from an old sidewalk, patio, or driveway. It's an ecologically friendly choice that keeps old concrete out of the landfill. A sledgehammer or jackhammer can be used to bust up existing concrete paving into flagstone-like pieces. Sometimes concrete contains rebar (steel reinforcing bars); if so, you'll need to cut through it to make the urbanite usable as paving. Alternatively, check Craigslist or the Freecycle Network for free or inexpensive local sources of urbanite. Green-minded homeowners who are having an old patio or driveway removed will sometimes offer their broken concrete to anyone willing to haul it away, saving it from the landfill.

Irregularly shaped flagstone and urbanite can be pieced loosely or more closely to make a paved surface, with decomposed granite or coarse sand filling the gaps between pieces. These gaps are what make the paving porous. When it rains, water seeps into the gaps and percolates into the soil below. Wide gaps between stones can even support a groundcover of thyme or other low-growing plant for a ribbon of green and better water-absorbing ability.

To install flagstone or urbanite paving, dig out sod and soil to a depth of about 8 inches. Spread 4 inches of paver or road base (essentially crushed stone of varying sizes, which compacts to a firm surface; it can be purchased by the bag at home-improvement stores or in bulk from landscape supply yards), sloping it gently away from any structures so that runoff won't pool against the foundation, and use a tamper or vibrating plate compactor to compact the material. Install your edging, which may be stone blocks, brick, concrete pavers, flexible steel landscape edging, or bender board. Next, spread a couple of inches of coarse builder's sand across the space, and then begin laying your flagstone or urbanite. Use 2- to 3-inch-thick pieces that are as large as you can manage with the aid of a wheelbarrow or furniture dolly. Thinner pieces may shift on the sand base and pop up in an unmortared patio. Thicker pieces will stay put. If your winters are cold enough to produce frost heave, follow local recommendations regarding the depth of excavation and paver base.

To avoid a tripping hazard, lay your stone flush with the top of your edging material. As you add each piece, use a level to ensure that you're creating a level, gently sloping surface; the gentle slope keeps water from pooling on the surface. If using natural stone, keep in mind that each piece will not be exactly the same thickness, so you'll need to add sand or scoop it away as necessary to level the stones as you go along. Also, whether working with stone or urbanite, be sure to juxtapose larger slabs with smaller, filler pieces. You don't want to use up all the big pieces at the start of the project, only to be left with small filler pieces when finishing the far side.

Once the flagstone or urbanite has all been laid, use coarse sand or decomposed granite to "grout" between the pieces. Using a push broom, sweep the sand or DG into the cracks and gently wet it with a fine mist of water. As the sand or DG settles, keep adding more until the grouting material is level with the paving. As a final step, carefully spray the stone or urbanite with a stream of water to wash away caked dirt and uncover the natural beauty of stone or the clean look of concrete. If you wish, urbanite can be stained for a more natural look.

For a classic, more formal look than flagstone or urbanite paving, bricks, concrete pavers, and cut stone make good choices. Sure, the spaces between these materials are narrower than with flagstone, but laid on a bed of gravel and sand, they still allow water to filter into the soil. Installation is essentially the same as detailed for flagstone and urbanite.

This circular stone patio is mortared with blue-gray river rock that evokes rivulets of water.

pervious concrete

A solid pavement that actually drinks up rainwater and allows it to percolate into the soil may sound too good to be true. But pervious concrete, also known as porous concrete, does just that. Whereas concrete is a mixture of cement, aggregate (small rocks), and sand, pervious concrete contains cement, larger aggregate, and no sand. Pocked with voids, the resulting paving looks more textured and less smooth than regular concrete—picture an orange peel rather than apple skin—but still makes a solid walkable or driveable surface. It can be poured in place like traditional concrete paving, or it can be installed in paver form. Either way, this is a job for a professional contractor who is experienced with pervious concrete paving.

Whether poured or laid as pavers over a thick layer of gravel, pervious concrete traps and holds rainwater until it can be absorbed by the soil underneath. Because it is so porous, pervious concrete can become clogged by debris, rendering it as impervious as regular concrete. Therefore, you'll need to plan on regular maintenance to keep it clean. Promptly remove leaf litter and other debris, including road salt, and clean the paving with a wet-vac twice a year. Because of these cleaning requirements, you'll want to consider carefully whether this type of paving is right for you. For instance, if you use your driveway to receive an annual truckload of compost or mulch for the garden, pervious concrete won't be a good choice. It's also important not to install it alongside your house foundation, since stored water can lead to foundation damage or basement leaks. Nor is it designed to absorb extra runoff beyond what falls on it directly, such as from an overhanging roof or nearby hillside. In such cases you may need to excavate a swale or dry stream next to the paving to move extra runoff away and into a rain garden. Aside from these constraints, pervious concrete can be a good choice for those who want a solid surface that absorbs more water than most other types of paving. For residential use, it's best suited to paving relatively flat driveways and parking areas that would otherwise shed water from the lot.

Above: Flagstones "mortared" with decomposed granite pave a casual patio.

Left: Cut limestone set in gravel makes an elegant and water-permeable front walk.

irrigation without irritation

In a perfect world, rain would fall gently and as regularly as needed—and just before dawn so as not to keep us indoors all day. Drought and irrigation systems would be unknown. And we and our gardens would all live happily ever after.

In reality, rain doesn't always come when needed. Sometimes it rains a lot early in the season and later not at all. Some years rainfall measures at average levels; other years it floods or the rains never come. Drought raises the specter of plant death and garden destruction, even when the garden contains native and well-adapted plants. The fact is, all plants, even cacti, need water. Some species can go longer than others without it, but eventually it must rain or you must water to sustain a garden, no matter where you live.

Yes, but plants in nature live without human intervention, so why can't gardens? It's a reasonable question. The answer is that a garden is not natural. It is a human creation set apart from nature through plant choice, fencing, mown lawns, streets, and the simple act of weeding. To paraphrase author Michael Pollan, a garden turns the prose of the natural landscape into poetry. Even if a garden blends with the surrounding landscape, the gardener imposes his or her will through the selection and arrangement of plants, deciding whether to allow them to reproduce and spread and

A soaker hose weeps via tiny pores along its length.

determining when and how they shall be pruned. If you don't see the difference between nature and a garden, just stop maintaining one and see how fast nature swallows it up.

A realistic understanding of local climate and rainfall patterns, smart plant choices, water collection, and other water-saving practices as detailed throughout this book are essential to creating a garden that doesn't need babying with the hose. After all, water is a precious resource—*the* most precious resource in the world—and we must be thoughtful about its use and conserve as a matter of course. But we need not give up gardening to do so. Even ornamental gardens, which some might dismiss as mere frivolity in water-challenged climates, do much good: they provide green spaces in an increasingly urbanized world, offer habitat and safe stopovers for wildlife, cool the air and shade the soil, entice us outdoors, and bring the joys of art, creativity, and the beauty of nature to their owners, visitors, and passersby.

Having established that gardens are worthwhile creations that need at least occasional watering, let's talk about irrigation, a sometimes dreaded word that brings to mind tangled hoses, expensive sprinkler systems, watering-can lugging, gopher-chewed tubing, and water waste. How do water-saving gardeners make irrigation as efficient and useful as possible?

First, before turning on the hose, evaluate whether the garden needs to be watered. Newly planted gardens, even those with natives or plants labeled drought tolerant, need regular, perhaps frequent watering. Freshly popped into the ground, new plants have a root ball that's only as big as the pot they arrived in. Weeks or months may go by before their roots tentatively start spreading and pushing deeper into the soil, searching for moisture and nutrients, and until then they must be given regular water as appropriate, depending on the type of plant and your climate. For example, dry-loving plants like yucca or agave might drown if saturated by daily watering, but they may appreciate weekly or every-two-week watering if you're trying to establish them during a broiling, rainless summer. It's a common and expensive mistake to forget to water new plants, or to water inadequately, with a quick blast from the hose that merely wets the leaves or the soil's surface rather than the deep, root-reaching soak that new plants need. On the other hand, it's also easy to overwater, and, unhelpfully, the symptoms can look the same. Therefore, check soil moisture several inches down before watering, either by sticking your finger deeply into the soil or by using a soil moisture gauge.

watering wisely

Advice on how much to water your garden is completely useless unless offered by someone who knows what kinds of plants you're growing, what your soil is like, whether your lot is sloping or flat, how much sun or shade your garden receives, how hot it is during the day and overnight, and how much it's rained recently. In other words, *you* are in the best position to judge when your garden needs water, not an expert from another part of the country and not even your friend who has a beautiful garden across town. It's up to you to learn what your garden needs and when, just like you learn how to care for a puppy or a baby. Take heart, though: a garden is much easier to care for than either of those. For one thing, it won't wake you up in the middle of the night!

Experience will teach you how to "read" your plants for signs of thirst. As soon as your garden is planted, make a point of walking through it every day, preferably in the morning, and really look at each plant. You're training your eye to recognize what's normal and what's not, which will help you catch any problems early on. (As a side benefit, you'll also enjoy the daily events—new flowers opening, berries ripening, birds flitting—that are among a garden's greatest pleasures.) Even if you have regular maintenance help, you are the one living with your garden and are in the best position to see what's going on with it. You also have invested your money and likely your own labor in its creation, so you want to make sure your garden's watering needs are met.

Plants with adequate moisture look full, not wilted, and their leaves are relaxed, uncurled, and not crispy or brown at the tips. Wilted plants may be showing their thirst. To be sure, poke your finger several inches into the soil around the base of the plant. If the soil is dry at the depth your finger can reach, and if it's a new plant, it probably needs a good soak. Remember, established plants can go longer without watering because their roots extend much deeper into the soil. You can test soil moisture in an established garden by sinking a shovel into the soil (away from plants, so as not to cut into their roots), pulling back on it, and feeling the soil for moisture; if it's dry at a depth of 6 to 12 inches, you probably should water. Don't make baby plants wait for a drink. However, when they're older, like children, they can be taught to "get their own cup of water" by growing deeper roots. How? By watering deeply and less frequently so that plants don't just grow roots at the surface, waiting for their daily drink. Less frequent, slow watering will teach them to search out cool, damp soil at deeper levels.

While it's true that many plants in temperate regions will grow very well with short bursts of more frequent irrigation that keeps soil evenly moist, that's not always an option for those in drought-challenged climates, where cities often enact watering restrictions that limit outdoor watering to once a week, once every two weeks, or even once a month. Better to start off training your plants to grow deep roots than to baby them well into maturity and find they can't survive when the going gets tough—that is, when drought comes and watering restrictions kick in. As pioneering desert garden designer Steve Martino says, if the water is shut off, your garden shouldn't die. My addendum to that is, at least not without a fight. Lack of water will kill every plant sooner or later—sooner if you live where rain is generally plentiful or if you water daily and suddenly the tap in the sky or on your house dries up. Therefore it's important to be clear-eyed about climate, even as you dream big for your garden. The best way to save water is to plant appropriately for the region in which you live, especially keeping in mind its rainfall patterns, average high temperatures, and soil type. Planting a verdant lawn and moisture-loving azaleas if you live in the Southwest, for example, is just asking for heartbreak.

easier irrigation

Irrigation is much easier to manage when all the plants in a particular bed need the same amount of water. If you take thirstiness into account when choosing your plants and group together those with similar watering needs, you'll save yourself a lot of work and water too. When water-loving plants are mixed with dry-tolerant plants, you're setting yourself up for extra work. You'll have to either lug around a watering can or drag the hose to spot-water

Shrink thirsty lawn to what you really need. This small swath of lawn is surrounded by a low-water garden mulched with gravel.

the thirsty plants, or you'll end up watering the whole bed more than most of the plants need, putting them at risk for rot or, at the least, wasting water on plants that don't need it. Instead, group thirstier plants close to your house or patio, where you can readily admire them, keep an eye on their watering needs, and have easy access to a water supply. Group plants that can go longer without water farther from the house, and plant those that can thrive without any supplemental watering at the outer edge of your garden. Your garden will be easier to maintain, and plants that need more attention will be easier to reach. On top of that, you'll water less since you'll be irrigating only those plants that really need it. (For more information, see chapter 8, page 141.)

Another way to reduce your irrigation is to reduce the area that needs water. This sounds obvious, but it's easy to overlook. Consider how much water is going where, whether it's money and water well spent, and whether you could add hardscape (again, that's nonplanted elements like paths, patios, and decks that give people a place to enjoy the garden) or natural areas to reduce irrigation needs. Sometimes in our enthusiasm for creating a garden we plant every square inch of the yard just chock-full of plants, leaving no room for patios, gazebos and arbors, and other spaces from which to enjoy our creation. Or we create beds that meander aimlessly in a hard-to-water wiggle. Or maybe your home's landscaping is just the builder's default solution, a wall-to-wall carpet of lawn that requires weekly or biweekly watering. Could you shrink your lawn to a small, usable space near the back door rather than maintaining a carpet of it, front and back, that never gets used? Could you install a large patio surrounded by drought-tolerant plants in place of lawn? Small patios work well in the front garden too, especially near the door, allowing you to take out even more thirsty lawn. (See chapter 6, page 115, for more information about reducing your lawn.) What about reshaping a rambling garden bed into a more compact garden with a bigger impact as well as an easier-to-water footprint? Perhaps you could lay more paths through your garden, which not only never need watering but also create a more inviting space.

in-ground systems

When altering existing landscaping to make a garden—perhaps replacing a lawn with a patio and planting beds—you'll need to make adjustments to any existing irrigation lines and sprinkler heads. Lawns, especially on large suburban lots, are commonly watered with in-ground sprinkler systems with pop-up heads that spray a large volume of water across a low-growing expanse. While this type of spray works well for lawns, it's not the most efficient way to water a garden made up of shrubs, perennials, and groundcovers of various heights, with deeper roots that need longer, slower watering rather than a surface-wetting spray. Plan to switch out your pop-up heads for taller shrub heads when you convert lawn to garden. Where you plant low-growing groundcovers like sedges, lilyturf, or other creeping or spreading plants, add height extensions called risers to your pop-up heads. If you change the layout of your garden beds, you'll also likely need to cap off unneeded heads, rearrange others, and reprogram your watering zones to reflect the needs of plants in your new beds. Plan to hire an experienced, licensed irrigation contractor to help you make the appropriate changes.

Make sure your spray heads are high enough to water your plants efficiently.

If you're planting a new garden, installing a programmable irrigation system can be an enormous help in keeping it watered, especially as it's getting established or if you live where watering restrictions do not allow daytime watering due to evaporation loss. This doesn't necessarily mean an in-ground sprinkler system, although that's a popular choice for those with a large lot in a hot climate. Such a system does have many advantages, such as programmable zones that allow you to deliver differing amounts of water to various parts of the garden. Spray heads, which should be mounted on risers for no-lawn gardens, can cover a sizeable area, which is useful for large gardens. Also, for gardeners who enjoy adding new plants or digging up existing plants and moving them around, a sprinkler system's sturdy PVC pipe, buried 8 to 12 inches underground, tends to deflect an errant shovel. In other words, you can dig to your heart's content without worrying too much about nicking or severing a watering line. The controller can be set to run early in the morning to reduce evaporation loss, or overnight, if your city doesn't allow daytime watering.

Of course, there are downsides to in-ground sprinkler systems, and the most significant are expense of installation and water waste. Because this type of irrigation system sprays water into the air rather than delivering it directly to plants' roots, much water can be lost along the way. Evaporation and wind take their portion, and runoff claims its share; either way, that's money going down the drain, and your plants don't receive the benefit of lost water. Also, watering foliage, especially overnight when it doesn't dry quickly, can lead to fungus, powdery mildew, or other diseases. Human error is also possible: it's all too easy to set the controller on the automatic setting and forget about it, even allowing it to water during a rain. To make the most of your system and reduce water loss, rely less on the automatic settings and adjust how much and when you water based on rainfall, temperature, wind, and time of year. Don't just set it and forget it, tempting as that may be. Keep your system turned off and evaluate each week, before turning it on, whether you really need to water, taking any rainfall into account and checking soil moisture. Consider installing soil moisture and rain sensors that detect when watering isn't needed, and keep your system from running then. Adjust it as needed, lessening watering time during cooler seasons and turning it off entirely

during winter or in wetter seasons. Otherwise, maintenance is minimal, although in cold climates the pipes must be blown out and drained for the winter.

An ornamental spinning sprinkler simply attaches onto the end of a hose.

hose-end sprinklers

On the simpler end of the spectrum, the most common method of irrigation is the hose-end sprinkler head, which screws onto a garden hose and can be placed wherever you need to water. Its biggest advantages are affordability and ease of use, and it's particularly handy if you need to water only a small area and only occasionally. Unfortunately, it can easily lead to the same kind of water waste as an in-ground system—evaporation and wind loss and runoff—as well as foliar disease. Irrigate early in the morning on a calm day to maximize the water that reaches your plants' roots. Watering in the heat of the day, especially at midday or in the afternoon, is wasteful because evaporation sucks up much of it before it can soak into the soil. To avoid wasting water by accidentally letting it run too long—which is

the water-saving garden

very easy to do—buy a hose timer and use it every time. Battery operated, a hose timer simply screws onto the faucet, and then you screw the hose onto the timer and program it to run for a set time. It'll turn off the water automatically at the right time, saving you the expense, guilt, and waste of a forgotten sprinkler left running overnight.

drip irrigation

To avoid water loss from wind and evaporation, reduce the likelihood of runoff, and prevent diseases triggered by wetting leaves, use an irrigation method that delivers water directly to plants' roots, where it's needed: drip irrigation. The easiest, cheapest, and least technical way to use drip irrigation is simply to lay soaker hoses in your garden beds, circling the plants within their drip zone (the space between the trunk or main stems and the outer perimeter of foliage). A soaker looks like a regular hose (although it's generally black, gray, or brown rather than green, to blend with the soil) but with one critical difference: it has weeping pores along its length. When you turn it on, water seeps through the pores and delivers water in a slow soak, which helps prevent runoff. Water won't evaporate or blow away either because it's not sprayed into the air. You can connect two soakers together to water a larger garden bed, provided your water pressure is sufficiently high. However, you'll get a more even distribution of water by using one soaker hose at a time.

Soakers are particularly handy for difficult-to-water areas like the narrow strip alongside the driveway. Be sure to snake your soaker hose through all the plants in a garden bed so that they all get watered, but keep the hose pulled away from tree trunks and the base of shrubs to prevent rot and disease. Later on, when planting or transplanting, remember to scrape away the mulch and locate the hose before putting shovel to soil; it's easy to accidentally cut a soaker hose with a shovel, necessitating replacement or time-consuming repair. Generally made of recycled rubber, soakers tend to degrade in direct sunlight, and they look unsightly anyway, so cover them with a light layer of mulch. When you run the soaker, use a hose timer that turns it off after a specified time. As always, check the moisture of your soil

Gardens offer refueling stopovers for migrating wildlife like monarch butterflies.

Left: A micro sprayer on a drip system delivers a targeted spray of water just above ground level.

Right: Drip tubing is laid in a new bed, with emitters delivering water directly to the plants.

to make sure water is soaking several inches deep. Because water seeps out slowly, you may need to run the soaker hose longer than you'd expect.

Soakers are useful and water saving, but drip irrigation can be more efficient with the use of flexible plastic tubing and emitters that run to each plant. A sophisticated drip system, unlike a soaker hose, can water a larger garden and delivers water directly to each plant, with less water waste. A well-designed drip system uses 20 to 50 percent less water than an in-ground sprinkler system, according to the Environmental Protection Agency, and can save as much as 30,000 gallons per year—a big savings of both water and money. Its ground-level delivery of water prevents runoff and water loss due to evaporation and wind. Drip irrigation is so efficient that it's often exempt from municipal watering restrictions. It's significantly cheaper to install than an in-ground system, with parts readily available at home-improvement stores, and since it's DIY-friendly, labor costs are not necessarily incurred. A do-it-yourselfer can set it up in a day, with no digging required. Because a drip system waters only the plants you run it to, weed seeds don't get watered and fewer weeds grow. It's customizable too: plants with higher watering needs can be served by adding extra emitters or using emitters with a greater flow rate, and the entire system can be set up with a programmable controller to turn it on and off automatically.

So why doesn't everyone use it? Well, there are some drawbacks, and it's not ideal for every situation or every gardener. Drip systems aren't appropriate for lawns or spreading groundcovers because they don't broadcast water in an even spray. Gophers and other wildlife can be attracted to the water in the tubing and chew holes in it. The tiny holes in tubing and emitters can get clogged, choking off water to plants, and because they're hidden under a layer of mulch and the water doesn't spray, you may not notice there's a problem until a plant shows signs of drought stress. In cold climates, drip tubing must be pulled up at the end of each growing season, stored for the winter, and set up anew each spring. If you're a digger with a penchant for moving or adding plants, drip irrigation can be a pain to work around, and it's easy to accidentally cut through the tubing with your shovel.

Use drip in smaller gardens that contain ornamental trees, shrubs, perennials, and ornamental grasses—not a sweeping lawn—and in vegetable beds. Lay porous tubing around trees and shrubs within their drip zone but not up against the trunk or stem. Spread a light layer of mulch over the tubing to protect it from the sun, as UV rays break down the plastic and reduce its life expectancy. And be sure to use a fine-mesh filter where the tubing connects to the outdoor faucet to keep dirt particles from clogging the tiny weep holes. If you make a commitment to regular maintenance and are willing to be careful when digging, drip irrigation pays off in a lower setup cost, lower water bills, and increased watering efficiency.

WATERING DOS AND DON'TS

Whatever type of irrigation you use, follow these water-saving tips to increase efficiency and reduce water loss.

---

* Evaluate soil dryness and weather before turning on the hose or the irrigation system. Don't automatically water twice or three times a week, rain or shine.

* If you use an automatic irrigation system, turn it on manually rather than running it on autopilot—or at least decide, on a weekly basis, whether to set it to run. Manually turning it on means you'll stop and think about whether it's necessary to water, and for how long, rather than setting it and forgetting it.

* Use a timer to turn off the water. It's easy to forget that a hose is running or the drip system is turned on. A timer prevents accidental and wasteful overwatering.

* Water in the predawn or early morning, not during the heat of the day when evaporation loss will be high. Evening, when it's cooler, is also a good time to water, although wetting foliage overnight, when it can't quickly dry, can lead to fungus, mildew, and other plant diseases in humid climates.

* Water on calm days to reduce water loss due to wind.

* Put a rain gauge in your garden so you always know how much rain you've gotten and can adjust irrigation accordingly. Place your rain gauge in an exposed location, not under a tree or roof overhang.

* If your soil is dry, water on two shorter cycles rather than one long run in order to reduce runoff. The first cycle "wets the sponge," and during the second cycle, the water can be absorbed by the moistened soil.

* Turn off your irrigation or at least reduce how often it runs in winter, when plants are dormant. Plants don't need as much water then as they do in hot weather or when they're actively growing.

* Inspect your in-ground irrigation system in early spring for leaks, clogged emitters, broken spray heads, and spray heads that are watering the street or driveway. Check drip systems for leaks or clogs in the tubing. Fix any problems right away, before you need to begin watering. Do another check of an in-ground system in early summer, making sure that plants haven't grown into the path of a spray head. If so, trim the plant or adjust the spray head.

Soaker hoses wound through a vegetable bed deliver water along the length of the hose.

the nitty-gritty on soil and mulch

Soil is something we don't give much thought to—
it's just dirt, right?—until we become gardeners,
and then we obsess about it.

Sandy-soil gardeners grumble about sieve-like conditions. Those with sticky clay that turns rock-hard in summer fret that their plants will either drown or parch. Stocking the garden shed with pickaxes instead of shovels, gardeners with rocky soil scowl over plant labels that include the words "evenly moist soil." I understand this soil obsession all too well. Before the ink was dry on the purchase contract for my current home, I emailed the sellers to ask about their dirt. *How deep can you dig before you hit rock?* I inquired. *Would you say the soil is clayey or stony?* And, a bit madly: *Just wondering, but do you know if compost was ever brought in?* They surely wondered whether I was planning to move into the house or the back yard.

Knowing your soil is the second-most important step in creating a water-saving garden, right after knowing your climate. Your garden's soil type directly impacts which plants you can grow in it. Aside from how well or poorly it holds moisture, soil is categorized by its pH level. Some soils are neutral (pH 7); others are acidic (pH below 7) or alkaline (pH above 7). Broadly speaking, wetter parts of the country, like the East Coast and Pacific Northwest, have acidic soil. Dry regions like the Southwest have alkaline soil. While your plants aren't chemists—and neither must you be—pH

New beds prepped and mulched in summer can wait until fall for planting.

affects how well they're able to absorb nutrients from the soil. Many plants prefer neutral to slightly acidic soil but will tolerate slightly alkaline soil. However, some plants will thrive in only one type. It's wise, therefore, to have at least a general idea of whether the soil in your region tends to be acidic or alkaline; your local extension office or a trusted local nursery will be able to tell you. Can you change your soil's pH? The short answer is no. The long answer is, only in a very limited way, by repeatedly (forever) spreading soil amendments around the plants that need intervention. To my mind, this is a waste of time, money, and effort. My philosophy regarding soil pH—to use a Southern idiom—is that you ought to dance with the one that brought you. Plant for the soil type you have, not the soil type you wish you had.

Happily, there's really no such thing as *bad* soil (unless we're talking about human-caused contamination or degradation) because all types of soil occur naturally, and there are plants for every type. Whether your soil is deep clay, glacial till, fertile loam, or shovel-breaking caliche, if you choose plants that naturally grow in the kind of soil you have (and are climate-appropriate), they will thrive. These include native plants and adapted exotics that have proven themselves well suited to your area, aren't invasive, and don't require pampering. Native plants make your garden look like it belongs in the wider natural landscape. They provide a sense of place that's especially welcome in an increasingly homogeneous world. Moreover, they are innately connected to the climate vagaries of your particular region and have evolved appropriate survival mechanisms that other plants may not have.

Of course gardening, like love, isn't always rational and can be driven by deeply romantic or sentimental impulses. Perhaps you long to grow your mother's favorite rose, or lavender that makes you feel like you're on vacation in Provence. Maybe you lust for the drama of a spiky agave, or you unabashedly want to grow every plant you can get your hands on. Who's to deny love? Love of plants motivates many of us to start gardening, and water-saving gardeners are no different. I'm not interested in a dogmatic approach to gardening, where one is made to feel guilty for growing some cherished exotics instead of only natives or for choosing to baby a few

Exotic *Aloe barbadensis* and native palo blanco trees (*Acacia willardiana*) thrive in this Arizona garden's rocky, dry soil.

thirsty plants in a garden that's largely water-thrifty. I say, go ahead and plant those sentimental or coveted plants that need special soil (pots or raised beds are good ways of accomplishing this) or other intensive attention, and enjoy them to the fullest. But in your quest to make a garden that isn't wasteful of water, for the majority of your garden, let your soil type be your guide and choose native and adapted plants that grow well without copious watering or soil amendments. You'll be nurturing your love of place and love of the Earth, which are equally powerful gardening motivators.

While planting for the soil you have, there *are* things you can do to your soil to help it hold water or, conversely, drain faster. Let's get down to the nitty-gritty details and talk dirt.

add compost—but only in certain situations

You can tell a lot about your soil simply by digging a hole—or by trying. *Can* you dig a hole? If not, do you hit unyielding rock, or hardpan that softens after a rain? If you pour water into the hole, does it hold water or drain quickly? Clay soils are mucky after a rain but dry out and even crack during drought. Sandy soils act like sieves; water passes right through. Rocky soils and caliche (cement-like mineral deposits) are hard to dig, tend to contain few nutrients, and impede root growth. While plants do exist for each type of soil, extreme conditions can limit you to a narrow range of plants. In many cases, it can be useful to apply compost and mulch for added fertility and water-holding capacity, allowing you to grow a greater diversity of plants. After all, there is value in plant diversity, specifically in increased resistance to disease and in creating a garden that supports wildlife. And because love of plants is why many of us garden, you may wish to make your soil hospitable to a greater variety. Adding organic material—compost or aged manure—to clay soil loosens tightly packed particles, allowing air and water to penetrate more easily. Added to sandy soils, compost helps retain water, giving plants a longer drink before draining away. And it provides essential nutrients and water retention in poor, rocky soil.

If you garden in temperate regions of the country that were once or are still forest, prairie, or wetlands—anywhere plants naturally grow densely and leaf litter, pine straw, or other organic materials cover bare soil—use compost to build up your soil, making it fluffier, more fertile, and better able to deliver water to plants' roots. Annually spreading a few inches of compost on your garden beds in early spring, when plants are cut back and ready to put out new growth, is a time-honored way to boost your garden's growth and remedy clayey or sandy soils. But if you garden in arid or desert regions— anywhere plants grow individually, with gravelly soil in between—or if you grow dry-adapted native plants, save your money and your back and don't add compost. Dryland and desert plants—agaves, cacti, Mediterranean shrubs, and the like—have evolved to grow in rocky, nutrient-poor soils. They not only don't thrive but may rot in rich, composted soil. At best they'll grow spindly, thin foliage, bloom poorly, and die much sooner than they would in appropriate conditions. When planting, break up the soil at least twice as wide as the plant's pot (choose smaller pot sizes to make planting easier on you and the transition less stressful for the plant), and use existing soil to fill the hole around the plant. Don't add compost. Spread a layer of gravel as mulch to keep the roots cool and help the soil retain moisture without overwetting. Of course, if you wish to plant nondesert species in

Clockwise from top:
Excavation can reveal
rocks under the topsoil.

Caliche and limestone
are common in the
Southwest.

Clay soil can be
squeezed like Play-Doh
when wet.

the water-saving garden

a desert environment, you'll need to provide more-fertile soil. Raised beds and pots can be one way to indulge your plant lust without trying to amend your entire yard or committing to a much more water-needy garden.

keep soil structure intact

As any child digging in the dirt could tell you, soil is alive. Minerals, air, and water mingle with living and dead organisms to make up soil that supports plant life and, by extension, all life on earth. Invisible to the naked eye, a network of mycorrhizal fungi also lives in the soil in a symbiotic relationship with plants, increasing plants' ability to take in nutrients and improving their resistance to disease and drought. There's a lot we're still learning about the web of life in the soil, but it's already having an impact on recommended gardening practices. For example, traditional gardening methods cause regular soil disturbance through hoeing and tilling. Ever heard of double digging, which was once recommended for creating new planting beds? It's the onerous process of digging out topsoil and setting it aside, breaking up the soil beneath it and mixing in compost, and then replacing the topsoil. Nowadays double digging and tilling have fallen out of favor because we understand that turning the soil can destroy the web of mycorrhizal fungi that's so beneficial to plants. Plus soil disturbance encourages dormant weed seeds to sprout. Better to leave the soil structure intact and disturb it as little as possible. Instead, improve soil fertility by spreading compost over the surface rather than digging it in. Through the action of earthworms, rain, and other natural processes, the compost works its way into the soil to feed plants.

If soil is completely compacted, it may be impossible to dig, and water may run off when it rains rather than soaking in. In such cases, you may need to till in order to loosen the soil enough for planting. Limit tilling to the initial stage of garden prep, and work in compost while you're at it, if your plants will benefit from it. From then on, avoid tilling to let your soil structure rebuild.

In the cement-like caliche soils of the arid Southwest, planting holes often must be gouged out with an iron breaker bar, pickaxe, or auger. Tillers bounce along the ground, and any attempt at double digging would be futile. Don't even try! Break up native soil for the planting hole and use it as backfill. As discussed earlier, abstain from using compost when planting desert plants or arid-adapted natives.

avoid compaction

Space between soil particles allows oxygen and water to move through, which is essential for plant health. When soil gets compacted due to construction work (particularly common in new neighborhoods or after a remodel), vehicle parking, children's play, or excessive foot traffic, water cannot soak down to the roots of plants. Compacted soil on even a slight slope may shed water like an umbrella, causing erosion of precious topsoil in addition to wasted water. In such cases, it may be best to loosen the soil with a single tilling to open it up. Add compost at this time if appropriate for the type of plants you wish to grow. Then, if the weather is warm, wait a few weeks before planting to see if weeds appear. Tilling—and hoeing, for that matter—turns the soil and "plants" any weed seeds that were lying dormant on the surface. It also chops up roots and underground stems of certain lawn grasses and groundcovers, and the invasive ones will happily resprout, hydra-like, from each cut piece. Add compost and water, and you've created the perfect conditions for weed seeds to sprout, leading to more work as you must remove weeds before planting to keep them from colonizing the fluffy new soil of your garden. Waiting and weeding before planting will pay off in less work later, since weeding around new plants is much more difficult, and getting rid of weeds allows more water to reach the roots of your chosen plants.

If you're not in a hurry and can wait a year or more to plant, you can improve compacted soil by spreading 6 to 8 inches of compost, topping it off with a layer of mulch, and then just letting it sit. Over a period of months, rain and earthworms will work their magic, mixing compost into the existing soil and loosening it naturally. It may take multiple applications of compost and mulch and several seasons to significantly loosen your soil, but this process has the advantage of preserving existing soil structure and not exacerbating weed problems.

Preventive measures are important for keeping good garden soil or existing native soil from becoming compacted. Avoid walking in your planting beds, especially after a rain or irrigation. Lay narrow paths—flagstone, gravel, and mulch are good choices—throughout your garden to give you access for weeding and other maintenance. Also hold off on any new digging or planting until several days after a rain or watering. If you find that a section of your garden has become a cut-through for the mail carrier or visitors, add a path to direct traffic and use shrubs, a strategically placed bench, or fencing to block people from tromping through your planting beds.

mulch to retain moisture and improve growth

Bare soil is like a neon *Vacancy* sign for weeds. In regions with regular rainfall, plants quickly colonize bare soil, and opportunistic, fast-growing weeds are the first to move in. Foil them by spreading a 2- to 4-inch layer of organic mulch around your plants after planting—or before, if you are not able to plant right away after creating new beds. Organic mulch includes any type of plant material, like shredded hardwood, bark chips, pine straw, and shredded leaves. As these materials decompose, they feed the soil, plus they help keep plants' roots cooler in summer. Most important for a water-saving garden, mulch preserves moisture in the soil. This means plant roots have more time to absorb water after a rain or irrigation, and they won't need as much watering through the course of a growing season. Plant trials done with different kinds of mulches have shown that plants grow faster and bigger when mulched, no matter what type of mulch is used.

Mulch should not be allowed to touch or pile up against tree trunks or the crowns or stems of shrubs and perennials. Doing so invites rot as well as rodent and insect damage. So-called volcano mulching, in which mulch is piled high in a cone shape around a tree's trunk, is a common but harmful

Repeated leaf blowing will remove not only protective mulch but fertile topsoil.

practice especially beloved by landscaping crews. This kind of mulching can actually kill a young tree by preventing sufficient water from reaching its roots. Older trees can fall victim to boring and gnawing damage to their bark from insects and rodents, which use the mulch for cover. Instead of a volcano, create a donut of mulch around a tree, a ring 2 to 4 inches deep, with a generous gap in the middle around the trunk. Be sure to keep the mulch pulled away from the trunk, with a "donut hole" at least 6 inches from all sides of the trunk for small trees and 1 to 2 feet on large trees.

Too much mulch causes as many problems as too little. Mulch decomposes over time, but how long it takes depends on many variables: type of mulch, temperature, and rainfall and watering amounts. Some people (or their landscaping service) like to spread a few inches of mulch annually without checking to see whether it's really necessary—for example, if the mulch is thin, patchy, or entirely absent. If your existing mulch is intact and several inches deep, don't add more. Mulch that's laid on too thick can prevent water from reaching plants' roots.

On the other hand, if bare soil is showing only a few months after putting it down, try to figure out why. Was the initial layer too thin, and it's just worn away? Try spreading a thicker layer. Is it washing away when it rains?

This page: Wildflowers easily self-sow in gravel-mulched beds.

Opposite, clockwise from top: Shredded hardwood mulch stays put and suppresses weeds.

During Portland's rainy winters, bermed planting beds keep dry-loving plants from rotting.

Gravel mulch looks natural with dry-loving plants and aids drainage.

Try a different kind of mulch; shredded bark knits together and tends to stay put in a heavy rain better than bark chips, which float. Does the mulch inexplicably disappear after your yard-maintenance crew has visited? Your landscaping crew may do a great job of cutting and edging your lawn each week, but when they clean up the lawn clippings with a leaf blower do they also blow all the leaves and mulch out of your garden beds? I see this all the time. Leaf blowers are anathema to mulch. It's hard to blow leaves without sending mulch flying in the air too. One or two times of this and you're down to bare soil, and even that starts blowing away. What's left is hard-packed earth, devoid of the protective and nutrient-rich top layer of compost and mulch, with surface roots exposed to the sun. As you can imagine, this is not good for the health of your trees, shrubs, and other garden plants. The only solution is to talk with your lawn service about not blowing out the garden beds. Maybe they can rake out the leaves rather than blowing them. Or maybe you can live with the leaves for a while and then rake them yourself. Even better, shred them for composting or use them as mulch. A "messy" garden is better for plants and wildlife than a sterile, blower-scoured landscape.

In addition to organic, plant-based mulch, you can use inorganic materials as mulch, with the advantage that they won't decompose over time. Gravel, decomposed granite, and river rock are good options, and if a native stone is chosen, it helps the garden blend with the larger landscape, adding to its unique sense of place. Manmade mulch like crushed, recycled glass, which you can buy by the bag online and sometimes at local recycling centers, can be fun for a modern or eclectic garden, adding an unexpected, sparkly bit of color to a garden bed. Inorganic mulch theoretically lasts forever, making it tempting for those who dislike having to add new mulch periodically. Practically speaking, you'll still have to refresh even gravel and decomposed granite from time to time, as their small particles can sink into the soil, get washed away, or otherwise thin out. Desert and dryland regions are perfectly suited to rock and gravel mulches because it's what covers the ground naturally. In arid regions, where plants must duke it out for every available drop of water, desert plants have evolved to grow individually, with space between them. In a garden setting, which may be planted more densely, it still looks quite natural to spread locally sourced gravel or decomposed granite around your plants and let it flow into pathways as well, with no lines of hard edging to separate the garden from the paths.

In humid regions where plants naturally colonize bare soil, use of inorganic mulch must be carefully considered, and a regular weeding regimen must be accepted. Because gravel and decomposed granite do such a good job of keeping soil moist but also draining water away from the soil's surface, they make surprisingly hospitable nurseries for seeds of plants both desired and not. Your native wildflowers may sow thickly in decomposed-granite mulch, to your delight. But when it's Bermudagrass that sets up shop, you'll want to pull your hair out—because this grass is nearly impossible to pull out. What about laying weed block fabric underneath it? Nope. Weed seeds germinate readily in the top layer of gravel or decomposed granite, and once their roots grow deep enough to get tangled in the weed block fabric, they're even harder to pull. Save your money and skip the weed fabric.

Despite the weed issue, I don't want to discourage you from using inorganic mulch in wetter regions. It can be quite lovely and appropriate in certain kinds of gardens. Just be aware that it's a higher maintenance option and must be weeded regularly.

In arid regions, inorganic mulch is a natural, sensible choice. Plant-based mulches desiccate and rapidly break down in extreme sunlight, heat, and wind. Moreover, they look unnatural in a landscape that's inhospitable to forests and dense vegetation. Here, in a sun-washed, open, dry landscape, rock and gravel mulches truly belong. Locally sourced gravel and river rock serve to beautify gardens while helping conserve precious moisture in the soil. Weeds, which can plague humid-climate gardeners who use gravel mulch, are less of a problem where rainfall is sparse.

build raised beds and berms

Do you have rock, caliche, or compacted soil, which makes digging an exercise in frustration? Or do you, perhaps, have heavy clay soil that drains poorly and drowns the plants you want to grow? Building up soil in raised beds and berms can solve this problem. While it's not cheap to bring in quantities of good soil, it makes a huge difference to your plants, which can easily spread their roots and grow. Just as it does on a natural slope, water drains quickly from raised beds and mounded soil, creating good conditions for growing plants from dryland and desert regions, even if your climate receives much more rainfall. In any climate you may be able to reduce your water bill by growing plants that naturally prefer dry soil. Such plants often appreciate extra water that your climate may provide through natural rainfall so long as it doesn't saturate the soil at their crown or pool at their roots— conditions that bermed beds can help you avoid. Be sure to read plant labels carefully to ensure that any nonnative dryland plant you choose will be winter hardy in your climate. While summer rains rarely harm dry-loving plants in well-drained soil, winter moisture (rain or snow) can drown them.

Rectangular or square raised beds contained by low walls of rot-resistant wood, stone, steel, or brick are often constructed in order to grow vegetables, which require especially fertile soil. But they work well for all kinds of plants and are particularly suited to compact spaces and

Gravelly berms make hospitable conditions for dry-loving plants in this Raleigh, North Carolina, garden.

contemporary designs. Berms, on the other hand, being uncontained by vertical edging, work better in larger spaces. To avoid the "elephant's grave" look, in which a symmetrical, oval mound of soil sits lonely in the midst of lawn, sculpt a berm into a long, curved, and asymmetrical shape, with one side gently sloped and the other a bit steeper. Incorporate the berm into a larger garden bed to blend it into the natural contours of the property rather than allowing it to stand alone, rising like a brown-mulched burial mound in a sea of green grass. Cluster taller plants in the higher portion of the berm, at its center, but avoid planting in a straight, regimented line along the top of the ridge, which looks artificial. Instead, group plants in staggered, randomly spaced, high-and-low groups for a more natural effect.

Although it may be tempting to berm soil or build raised beds under trees, where masses of roots make digging difficult and soil is perennially parched, resist the urge. Trees rely on a fragile network of surface roots to obtain moisture and nutrients, and these are easily smothered by piling soil or even excessive mulch on top. Between half and three-quarters of a tree's feeder roots grow to a depth of only 1 foot, and these can spread out far beyond the

the water-saving garden

Wood-framed raised beds define a large vegetable garden.

canopy of leaves. Look up at your tree's canopy, mentally trace its diameter on the ground, and widen it by 1 foot per diameter-inch of the trunk: this is the root zone that must be protected. An inch or two of compost is generally considered okay, even beneficial, in the root zone of a tree, and a 2- to 4-inch layer of mulch is recommended for preserving soil moisture and increasing fertility (use inorganic gravel for desert trees). But adding extra soil to a tree's root zone can be harmful, even fatal. Therefore, locate berms and raised beds a safe distance away from your trees.

There's one more very good reason to consider berming soil or building raised beds. If you live in an older urban neighborhood, your soil could be harboring contaminants like lead (from vehicle exhaust and paint flaking off old houses), asbestos (from old house siding), coal ash (from the days of coal furnaces), or arsenic (from pressure-treated lumber). Even in suburban or rural locations, nearby train tracks, highways, power plants, gas stations, or other industrial business can leave a mark on the soil long after they're gone. For ornamental plants, this isn't really an issue, but if you plan to grow edibles, clean soil in elevated planting beds is a prudent choice. The necessary depth depends on the type of edibles you plan to grow, but a conservative guideline is 18 to 24 inches. Line the bottom of the bed with landscape fabric before filling with good soil in order to keep your plants' roots from growing into existing, potentially contaminated soil.

throw some shade
and shoot the breeze

In hot-summer and high-altitude climates, the sun can
seem like the Death Star, capable of frying tender
plants, drying out the soil, and sending the gardener
running for the shade.

Plants can't run for the shade, but we can plant them to take advantage of
shade cast by houses, walls, fences, and hedges. We can also give them relief
through strategic placement of shade structures and trees. The cooling shade
of a tree reduces air temperature by as much as 20 degrees Fahrenheit.
When a tree shades your house, this yields significant energy savings in
reduced cooling costs. It helps lower your outdoor water use too. Shielded
from baking sunlight by trees, arbors, shade sails, or other structures, the
soil retains moisture longer, giving relief to heat-stressed plants. Not all
plants need shade, of course—and many require full sun to perform best—
but in hot climates even many sun-loving plants appreciate afternoon shade
or light, filtered shade. Areas of shade allow you to grow a more diverse
garden, and it makes the garden more pleasant for the people who use it.
Therefore, when planning your water-saving garden, be sure to incorporate
shade for personal enjoyment, plant health, and energy and water savings.

For those in regions with cooler summers, shade isn't as big a concern. But
wind might be. Or maybe you contend with a double whammy of both wind

Steel arches offer
sturdy support for
shade-giving vines.

A painted stucco wall adds vibrant color to a desert garden and offers shade to plants and people.

and baking sun. Like a hair dryer set on high, wind sucks moisture right out of the earth and desiccates plants, especially those with large leaves. A windbreak can be the solution. Just as a sailor finds shelter on the leeward side of an island, plants on the nonwindy side of a hedge, wall, or building will be less parched than those exposed to the wind. By paying attention to seasonal wind patterns, you can plan for them and build walls or plant hedges to serve as windbreaks. Your protected plants will reap the benefit of increased moisture, and you'll enjoy your garden more without the annoyance of a ceaseless, drying wind.

Let's explore various ways of blocking sun and wind in order to conserve water in the garden.

Left: A wood-slat arbor attached to the house creates a shady dining space in a narrow side garden.

Right: A rustic ramada adds Southwestern style.

arbors

Arbors, pergolas, and ramadas, their Southwestern cousins, create shady, semi-enclosed lounging and dining spaces as well as permanent structure and focal points. Made of wood or steel, with a lattice or slatted roof, they filter sunlight and admit rain and breezes, making a kind of bridge between indoors and out. With the addition of a clambering vine, they offer even more shade.

Except when in pots, plants aren't usually planted beneath an arbor in home gardens. Still, plants in garden beds along the north and east sides of a shade structure do receive some beneficial shade as the sun tracks across the sky. A long pergola, perhaps running the length of a path or side of the garden, will cast quite a lot of shade, especially if draped with vines. To maximize the shade, align a long pergola along an east-west axis, with rafters oriented north-south. Plant vines that will clamber along the top and add even more sun protection. Position the pergola so that you have room along the north side for a garden bed. As the sun moves across the sky, the rafters will cast

lines of shade under the pergola, and the north-side garden bed will receive hours of filtered shade. The soil will stay cooler and moister here, offering an opportunity to grow plants that enjoy light shade and soil that holds more moisture.

It's worth mentioning that tall pergolas can be erected over garden beds to shield them from excessive sun in hot-summer climates. The Desert Botanical Garden in Phoenix and the Ruth Bancroft Garden in Walnut Creek, California, incorporate tall steel arbors to shade drought-tolerant but sun-scorchable succulents from the blistering afternoon sun. While such a structure may entail an expense only an endowed botanical garden would consider to shelter a special collection of plants, it does illustrate the versatility and usefulness of arbors in water-saving gardens.

shade sails

Shade sails are an increasingly popular option, especially in the Southwest and among fans of contemporary design. While fabric canopies have been used to shade marketplaces and courtyards since ancient times, the shade sail is a new version. Introduced to the United States from Australia and South Africa about 20 years ago, shade sails are graceful swoops of durable fabric, usually polyethylene, strung with high-tension cables between anchored steel or wooden posts; a sturdy tree trunk or a home's eave can provide an anchor point as well. Typically triangular in shape, like the sail of a boat, but also available in rectangular shapes, they may be hung in overlapping layers to maximize coverage. Water permeable, they allow some rainwater to drip through, as an arbor does. Suspended over a patio, deck, play space, or even garden beds, they filter sunlight to create bright shade (dark colors block more light) that's pleasant for people and many plants as well.

Triangular shade sails should be hung with one anchor point lower than the others so that water cannot pool, and for a dynamic appearance. The lowest point should be positioned high enough for head clearance. Rectangular sails are hung so that diagonal corners are at the same height, one pair

A pergola hung with vines offers hours of filtered shade.

Large shade sails cool
an outdoor classroom
at a xeriscape
demonstration garden
in Scottsdale, Arizona.

higher and the other lower, which creates tension and a narrow twist in the middle. A flat sail, by contrast, would not only lack visual appeal but also sag during a rain and collect leaf litter at other times. In planning a shade sail installation, be sure to consider the path of the sun. Position the sail so that its lower point is to the southwest of whatever you're shading so that you get more coverage in the hot afternoon than in the cooler morning. Posts must be quite strong and anchored with concrete footings to secure the sail under tension and when it's windy. If your region is prone to high winds, consult with your installer or the sail manufacturer for more information. Also, shade sails are not designed to support the weight of snow, so if you live in a cold-winter climate you'll need to take sails down before the first snow. Check your local building codes to see if there are any regulations regarding installation.

trees

Manmade structures like arbors and shade sails offer instant shade, but they can be expensive and require maintenance and periodic replacement

as materials age. If you plan to be in your home for some years and you have the patience, a well-chosen, appropriately placed tree eventually shades a much larger portion of the garden and possibly the house too. This reduces the burden on your air conditioner and lowers your electricity bill as well as cooling the soil and preserving moisture. Plant shade trees on the west and east sides of your house and garden for maximum cooling. Since hardscape like driveways, patios, and expanses of gravel absorbs heat and raises the air temperature, a tree planted to shade those areas will cool the garden too. It also matters whether a tree is evergreen or deciduous. In addition to greening up the bare winter season, an evergreen tree provides year-round shade, which may be welcome in a hot climate. In cooler climates, you might prefer a deciduous tree, one that loses its leaves in autumn, allowing the winter sun to warm the garden and brighten your home.

Do your research before buying a tree, and choose a native or well-adapted species that can survive on natural rainfall once established, with deep roots so it'll be less likely to compete with the rest of your plants for water. Know how tall and broad it will grow, and take into account power lines, other trees, structures, and other vertical competition for space. Never assume you

Left: A tree offers natural shading for a garden bench. A wall shelters the area even further.

Right: An ornamental tree may be the right size to shade a small garden without casting the whole yard into deep shade.

can simply prune a tree to fit a space where clearance is insufficient. Over-pruning or topping, in which the top of the tree is cut back, results in poor shape and stimulates unsightly, weak growth that makes a tree vulnerable to wind, snow, or ice damage. And even if you would never prune that way, the electric company might if your tree grows too close to the power lines. Therefore choose a tree with an expected mature height and width well within the available space, remembering that trees may grow a good dozen (or more) feet taller than their plant tags say they will. You should also avoid planting too close to your home's foundation or over a sewer line, to prevent damage caused by root growth. However, to shade the roof, a tree needs to be within about 20 feet of the house on the east or west side.

Many newer homes are built on small lots, and the yard that seems so spacious when you move in can quickly become overcrowded and as dark as a forest if you succumb to the temptation to fill the space with young trees. A sapling tree from the nursery looks deceptively tiny when first planted. But it takes only about five years for it to start filling out and providing significant shade. In ten years, your house may be completely obscured and your lawn and garden beds shaded out. For such lots, a single small or medium-sized ornamental tree, rather than a large shade tree, might be a better fit while still sheltering your home and patio spaces from the heat of the afternoon sun. On larger lots, you can cut loose by planting a mix of shade trees and smaller, ornamental trees. Unless you're designing a formal or contemporary garden, avoid the soldier effect of a line of trees evenly spaced and planted the exact same distance from the house. Shun, too, the bull's-eye appearance of a single tree placed smack-dab in the middle of the yard. Instead, plant a single tree several yards cattycorner to the left or right of center, leaving a clear, welcoming view of the front walk and door, and plant multiple trees in natural-looking clusters, spaced an uneven distance from the house and each other.

Trees of all sizes offer useful shade.

windbreaks: trees, hedges, walls, and fences

Trees not only cool the air and shade the soil but also provide shelter from the wind. Evergreen trees with dense branches that droop to the ground offer the most shielding, but even the winter-bare branches of deciduous trees disrupt and slow down wind currents. While a single tree protects a small area, a row of trees makes an effective windbreak for the whole garden and home, protecting vulnerable plants, reducing erosion, preserving soil moisture, and lowering your home's energy costs. Windbreaks work not by blocking the wind but by creating eddies and disturbances that slow down the wind and lift it up and over. The most effective windbreaks are actually porous enough to let air flow through, not solid like a wall. This is why a close planting of trees and shrubs works so well.

First, know your seasonal wind patterns. In many parts of the United States, the worst winds come in winter, howling south from the Arctic. But in Southern California, desiccating, hot "devil winds," the Santa Anas, blow in autumn and winter from the desert toward the coast, fanning wildfires along the way. Plant your windbreak on the windward side (where the wind is coming from) of your yard—generally on the north to block cold winter

Left: Evergreen Arizona cypress (*Cupressus arizonica*) makes an effective windbreak for hot, dry climates.

Right: Positioned properly, even a wire fence or trellis draped with vines can protect a garden from drying winds and give a little shade.

winds or on the east to block hot Santa Ana winds. On small urban and suburban lots, you'll need to plant along the property line. But if your lot is large, the rule of thumb is to plant a windbreak at a distance from the house that's two to five times the expected mature height of the trees. Trees should be planted close enough to each other that their branches touch as they mature, avoiding any large gaps that funnel the wind at even higher speeds. But you need not try to make a solid, impenetrable screen, as that can lead to a turbulent vacuum effect on the protected side. Choose trees with strong limbs and trunks that don't have a reputation for snapping in high winds. If you have the space, stagger your windbreak trees in an irregular zigzag

A painted wall and pergola set a cool-blue color scheme for a sheltered garden.

the water-saving garden

pattern so that they aren't lined up like soldiers, and use a mix of trees and shrubs for a more natural appearance. The depth of the windbreak is more important than height for channeling wind up and over the protected space in front of it.

A hedge, being shorter, can't protect the house as well as a windbreak of trees, but it can certainly shelter garden beds on the leeward (protected) side. A loose row of various types of shrubs, some evergreen and some deciduous, makes a natural-looking hedge, while a clipped line of a single species like boxwood or yew yields a more formal, traditional look. Either way, assuming you don't have a view to preserve, there's nothing prettier than a soft, green "wall" around your garden, creating a sense of enclosure and privacy and cutting off undesirable views of driveways, neighboring houses, and even one's own boring wooden or chain-link fence. When planting your garden, keep in mind that the north side of a hedge is shady and cooler all day. The west side is shaded in the morning but gets midday and afternoon sun; the opposite is true on the east side, which offers ideal conditions for many part-sun-loving plants. A garden bed on the south side of a hedge receives sunlight all day long as the sun travels over it from east to west.

Stucco walls shelter a sunken wildflower garden.

Like hedges, walls can provide narrow bands of shelter from sun and deflect wind from enclosed garden spaces. Brick and stone are classic wall-building materials in many parts of the country. In desert climates and in contemporary gardens, concrete block and stucco are more commonly used to enclose back yards and define garden "rooms." Because they absorb heat during the day and radiate it into the air at night, masonry walls create warm microclimates for nearby plants, especially if south- or west-facing. On the sunnier side of the wall, take advantage of the extra warmth by experimenting with plants considered slightly cold tender or that

An intimate patio garden is sheltered by a horizontal wood-slat fence.

thrive in reflected heat, like hardy desert species. On the cooler, shadier side, plant species that appreciate a little bit of extra moisture in the soil and afternoon shade.

Wooden fences and screens also prove useful for sheltering a garden, although they must be well anchored to stand up to gusty winds. Wood doesn't absorb and radiate heat like masonry does, so it's not useful in creating warm microclimates, if that's something you desire. Nevertheless, the shady side of a solid fence or vine-draped screen will remain cooler and the soil will hold more moisture than the exposed side, giving you more options for planting. In terms of windbreaks, even freestanding lattice screens (well anchored, of course) do a good job of slowing and diverting wind, making them well suited for enclosing a patio garden, giving privacy and shade in the process.

the water-saving garden

part three

PLANTING the water-saving garden

lose the lawn

Rolling like a green carpet from sea to shining sea, lawn reigns supreme as our national groundcover, surrounding nearly every house in every neighborhood across the country.

After all, it's inexpensive to install, basic maintenance is straightforward, and, when laid as sod, it's instantly "done." The downside, and it's a biggie, is that most lawns need lots of water to thrive. Also, traditional lawn upkeep—watering, mowing, edging, blowing, fertilizing, applying chemical weed inhibitors and pesticides—wastes energy and releases pollutants into the air and our groundwater. For these reasons, many people are now looking at lawns with a gimlet eye.

Where summers are mild and rain falls regularly, a lawn may not need supplemental watering. In the United States, these regions are limited to the Northeast, upper Midwest, and Pacific Northwest. Throughout the South, Midwest, Mountain West, Southwest, and California, however, scorching summers and weeks with no rain are commonplace. Most lawns require about an inch of water per week during the growing season, and if it doesn't come from the sky, it must come from the faucet. And in many cases, the lawn that requires so much water and mowing is rarely used. Because lawn is such a water guzzler, shrinking or replacing it with low-water substitutes

A sandstone patio and low-water garden give the owners a reason to linger in their back yard.

Native prairie plants
in a suburban front
garden glow with rich
color on an autumn
morning.

is an excellent way to save water in the landscape. Replacing even part of it can save thousands of gallons of water a year, not to mention reducing any pollutants from a gas-powered mower and chemical applications. Plus, the garden that you create in its place will give you more reasons to get outside than a lawn ever could, and this goes for children too. Birds, butterflies, bees, grasshoppers, and other wildlife will visit. Flowers will open and go to seed. Feathery grasses will beg to be touched. Trees and shrubs will change color in the fall. The cycle of the seasons will be a daily parade of enchantment in a way that a static lawn can never be.

Let's look at the many options that a water-saving garden can incorporate in place of thirsty lawn. Choose two or three (or more) of the ideas offered here. Make a plan, but remember that it's easier on the wallet and the back to work on one portion of your yard at a time rather than trying to do it all at once. Plus it gives you time to establish plants in one new section before moving on to the next.

shrink your lawn

Many people start a garden this way: they dig out a portion of lawn near the back patio or along the front walk to create a bed for flowers, shrubs, and perhaps a small tree. Over time they expand this bed by digging out more lawn, or they move to another section of the yard to swap out lawn for more garden space. You can use this approach to reduce your own lawn and create a water-saving garden. But think bigger than just one bed or even two. Size up your front or back lawn and think about how you use it—or if you use it at all. Do you need a lawn for children or pets? If so, how much space do they really need? Younger kids might need a small lawn for running around and kicking a ball, but older kids often spend their time on municipal sports fields rather than a lawn at home. A pet that enjoys patrolling the perimeter of the yard might not need a big lawn either so long as you leave room along the fence for him or her to run. Maybe you like the negative space that a lawn provides, a calm spot for the eye to rest amid a lushly planted garden. If so, could a low-water groundcover do the job instead, or a gravel patio? Is your front lawn *ever* used? If not, how about planting a low-water garden in its place?

Even if you think you might want to replace your entire lawn eventually, removing only a portion at first can be less scary, especially if you're worried about what your neighbors might think or you're not sure how to maintain

Before: The front lawn at designer Korina Petrozzi's house was rarely used, but sucked up 1,500 gallons of water per month.

After: With the lawn gone, Korina and her family enjoy a colorful, low-water garden and outdoor living space that needs only 140 gallons of water per month—90% less water than before.

BEFORE

AFTER

If you love the look of lawn, frame a small circular patch with a waterwise garden.

a no-lawn yard. Let me assure you: your neighbors may follow suit when they see how beautiful a water-saving garden can be, and you'll soon learn how to take care of your new plants just as you learned to care for a lawn, and you'll find it a lot more rewarding than pushing a mower.

One approach that works well for shrinking the lawn is to "push out" from the house with a patio and garden beds, relegating a much smaller lawn to the rear of a back yard or the street side of a front yard. A patio next to the house creates a paved openness, which, enclosed by garden beds, makes it inviting to step outside and provides accessible outdoor entertaining space. Nonflammable paving around the house also makes your home more fire resistant if you live in a region at risk for wildfires. The opposite approach also works well: keep lawn close to the house but, farther away, replace it with garden beds, a patio, a shade pavilion, a play set surrounded by cushioning pea gravel or bark mulch for the kids, or a combination of these. In both scenarios, you can easily eliminate half your lawn and gain attractive and useful outdoor spaces in the process.

Another way to reduce the lawn is to frame it as a focal point in a larger garden. This works especially well for those who like the negative space and cool, green restfulness that a lawn provides. For a formal look, shape the lawn into a rectangle or circle, and frame it with stone or brick edging to set it off from surrounding garden beds. Lead the eye and provide access with a clear path from the house to the focal-point lawn. If you can align it with your door or a main window overlooking the garden, you'll get even more of a wow factor out of it, and the framed lawn will draw you right out into the garden. If an informal garden is more your style, lay out a small comma- or amoeba-shaped lawn with broad curves, surrounded by garden beds. Lay a meandering stepping-stone path to reach it, and place a bench or a couple of Adirondack chairs in one of the broad curves. A small lawn that's framed to draw the eye amid a larger garden is particularly inviting and appealing, and your whole yard will feel larger, paradoxically, once you've created divisions of space between lawn and garden.

plant a native or ecological lawn

If you like the calm, uniform look of a sweeping lawn—or your homeowners' association (HOA) requires it—but you hate the watering, fertilizing, and mowing that traditional lawn grasses require, try a native or ecological lawn. Typically grown from seed but sometimes available as sod, these alternative lawns consist of a combination of native or adapted grasses and perhaps a few low-growing broadleaf species like clover and yarrow. Deep-rooted and growing in widening tufts rather than by creeping stolons or rhizomes (with the exception of buffalograss), they may take longer to fill in than traditional lawn grass, but once they do, they can subsist on normal rainfall and seldom require mowing—just once a month or a couple of times a year. They can even handle moderate foot traffic. Ecological lawns perform best when allowed to grow a little longer than a traditional lawn, and they appear slightly tufted with occasional mowing or meadowy with an annual mowing. I find this look immensely appealing and much more natural than a perfectly uniform lawn, but your HOA may disagree. Many HOAs in drought-prone regions are finally embracing less-thirsty options for landscaping by their residents, but just to be sure, consult your bylaws before making the switch. In less-restrictive neighborhoods or in eco-minded communities, you'll likely make converts of your neighbors once they see how little you're having to water or mow your new lawn.

Habiturf, an ecological lawn made up of grasses native to the southwestern U.S., needs little water or mowing.

U.S.-native buffalograss has long been the go-to choice for water-thrifty lawns in the hot and semi-arid Southwest and Great Plains, and new, denser, weed-resistant cultivars make it even more appealing. In sun it grows into a shaggy, blue-green carpet of thin-bladed grass that can be left long (it tops out at about 5 inches) or mowed monthly on a high setting. Forget watering it unless the rains completely shut off in summer, but even then it'll only go dormant until rain returns. In fact, since it needs only 1 or 2 inches of water a month to stay green (versus traditional lawn's 1 or 2 inches a week), it's easier to overwater than to underwater buffalograss. Being heavy-handed with the hose will make a buffalograss lawn vulnerable to weeds, so resist the urge to turn on the water. Buffalograss doesn't hold up well to heavy foot traffic, so it's not a good choice for a play lawn that will see a lot of use. But it works well for little-used back and front lawns.

More durable and weed-resistant lawn seed mixes for the Southwest and Southern Plains are being developed all the time. Thunder Turf, offered

by Native American Seed in Junction, Texas, and the promising new introduction Habiturf, developed by the Lady Bird Johnson Wildflower Center in Austin, are drought tolerant once established and need mowing only about once a month. Each consists of a blend of low-growing native grasses (including buffalograss) that matures into a dense, tufty turf. For cooler northern climates, fine-fescue grass blends like No-Mow Lawn Mix from Prairie Nursery in Wisconsin and Eco-Lawn from Wildflower Farm in Ontario thrive with only occasional water and mowing. Left long, these lawns offer a meadowy look; with once-a-month mowing, they blend easily into a neighborhood of traditional lawns. For added seasonal color and an even more meadowy look, try planting tall flowering bulbs in naturalistic clusters in a lawn that's seldom mown.

You can create an ecological lawn the old-fashioned way by allowing "weeds" like clover, dandelion, and horseherb (*Calyptocarpus vialis*) to pop up where they will; just mow everything to the same height if it starts

Native buffalograss makes a shaggy, touchable lawn for hot, dry climates.

looking weedy. You can also keep your existing lawn and simply choose not to keep it unnaturally green with heavy watering and fertilizing. Instead, allow it to go dormant (turn brown) during dry summers by withholding water. In most cases, especially with drought-resistant species like Bermudagrass and zoysia, lawn will green up again when the rains return. However, in very hot and dry climates benign neglect may actually kill off a lawn, leaving behind only undesirable weeds and bare dirt, so this approach works best in cooler, wetter climates.

If you decide to sow an ecological lawn, proper soil preparation is key to its success. Tempting as it may be, you can't simply toss eco-grass seed onto your existing lawn and expect good results. Existing grass and weeds must be completely eradicated and the soil tilled to a depth of between 3 and 8 inches (depending on the mix) to allow deep root growth. Add a layer of compost before seeding and water regularly at first to give the seedlings a good start. Your reward for all this prep work is a traditional-style lawn that blends with the neighbors', lets you park the mower in the shed, and gives your sprinkler system an extended vacation.

use grassy and creeping groundcovers

Once you start looking past traditional lawn grasses, all manner of alternative plants present themselves. For a grassy look, sedges, lilyturf, and small ornamental grasses carpet the ground in a swath of green that's reminiscent of lawn. In shady, damp locations where lawn struggles, moss quilts bare soil and even rock in evergreen velvet. For flowers and for foliage color and texture, try a creeping groundcover, low-growing shrubs and perennials, and succulents (in frost-free climates). Certain flowering species attract butterflies, bees, and hummingbirds, which are delightful to watch and add life to the garden. Whatever your site's conditions—sun or shade, moist or dry—you can find a ground-covering plant that needs less water than lawn and will enliven your garden with color, texture, and seasonal changes. Of course, no groundcover tolerates regular foot traffic as well as lawn grass, so these options are best suited to areas that are literally off the beaten track, where they can be admired but not trod upon. If people are

likely to walk on your groundcover planting, lay an accessible, visible path of large stepping stones or concrete pavers through it to protect your plants from wear and tear.

add paving

Those of us who love plants sometimes forget to leave room in the garden for hardscape—manmade garden features like paths, patios, decks, and other "people places." And yet such places are what make it comfortable to spend time in the garden. They can also take up a good deal of space formerly devoted to lawn, and they'll never need watering or mowing. The amount of hardscape in most people's yards is insufficient—maybe just a small concrete patio at the back door and a cramped, utilitarian walkway from the driveway or the street to the front door. Replace these with appropriately scaled patios and inviting walks, and you'll be able to remove some lawn in the process. Or, to save money, simply beef up what you already have, if it's in good shape, by enlarging existing patios and paths. The goal is not to pave over the garden but rather to thoughtfully add hardscape to the garden to make it more inviting and useable.

For curb appeal, lay a wide path from the street to the front door, and connect it with a side path from the driveway. Your path may be

Paving can take the place of lawn even in the front yard. Bordered by evergreen shrubs and trees, this limestone and pea gravel patio makes a gracious courtyard garden.

straight-lined contemporary or enticingly curvy, but whatever style you choose, make it wider than you think you need. Basic builders' walkways tend to be a measly 3 or 4 feet wide—ribbon-like dimensions that allow only enough room for an uncongenial, single-file approach to your door. For two people to be able to walk side-by-side, a walkway should be at least 5 or 6 feet wide. Lay out your proposed path with a couple of old watering hoses or by spraying contractor's marking paint (spray-paint cans that can be held upside-down to mark the ground, available in home-improvement stores). Then live with it for a few days, and walk it, to see if the proportions are right for your house. Keep in mind that a wide path may feel incongruously large when all that surrounds it is grass. But once you plant up the space around it, the path that looked so wide when newly installed will "shrink" as plants fill in and spill over the edges, and once your eye has other things to take in. Make the scene even more inviting and take out even more lawn by adding a small patio near the front door that offers room for a bench and a few eye-catching, focal-point pots. Use one type of paving material, whether stone, pavers, bricks, gravel, or poured concrete, to blend path and patio into one flowing space, creating a harmonious and gracious entry for your home. You can remove more lawn and make your front yard even more functional by laying a narrower secondary path to the side-yard gate, assuming your back yard is fenced.

In back, cast an appraising eye on your lawn to decide whether you really need all of it, or any of it. You can get rid of a big chunk by laying a generously sized patio either right off the back door or at the far end of the garden if that's where shade or a view can be found, creating a destination "room." Large patios can be affordable when paved with gravel or urbanite (broken pieces of concrete from old driveways or patios, which can sometimes be located cheaply or for free on Craigslist or the Freecycle Network). If neighbors are planning a remodel or relandscaping, they may be looking for an inexpensive way to dispose of busted-up concrete, and it doesn't hurt to ask. As a bonus, these materials let rainwater soak into the soil beneath rather than running off. Size your patio so that you can easily fit a dining table and chairs with room to walk around when people are seated and maybe a fire pit, if desired, surrounded by comfortable seating. You'll want room for potted plants to bring the garden closer to the house and maybe large containers for growing herbs or vegetables for the kitchen. In short, a large patio has many uses for entertaining, relaxing, and growing edibles near the kitchen, so resist the urge to skimp on size. It'll make your back yard more inviting, entice you and your guests outdoors, and give you a reason to eliminate a large portion of lawn with a low-water alternative. Consider running the patio along the entire width of your home, especially if you have exterior doors from multiple rooms—say, the kitchen and the living room—or if you might like to replace a living room window with double French doors to give better access to the back yard and make it easier to entertain outdoors. This is a classic French look—think of old stone farmhouses in Provence, where a gravel court flows out from the house, and a farm table and chairs under leafy shade trees invite outdoor dining on warm summer evenings. And if you live where wildfires are an annual risk, installing hardscape up against the house (stone, gravel, or concrete, not flammable wood) is a good way to create a fire barrier to protect your home.

If you have an existing patio that's uncomfortably small but too functional to tear out, and if it's located on relatively flat ground, consider enlarging it by extending an apron of gravel, unmortared flagstone, or other paving around the patio's outer edge. You can double or triple your patio's size this way and change a boring, square slab of concrete into a curve-edged entertaining space or, like a Mondrian painting, extend its rectilinear geometry into the garden with a grid of regularly spaced concrete pavers set in gravel. By using what you have and adding to it, you'll have the satisfaction of keeping material out of the landfill and saving money.

When installing paving, keep in mind that a water-saving garden retains as much rainwater and runoff as possible, holding it on-site to rehydrate the soil and to water the spreading roots of trees and other plants. Therefore try to choose materials that allow water to pass through, rather than impervious materials that shed water into storm drains. Pervious paving includes gravel; decomposed granite; unmortared flagstone, urbanite, pavers, and bricks; and pervious concrete and asphalt. Among these options, some are more pervious than others. Water passes more easily through loose gravel, for example, than it does through compacted decomposed granite, and it seeps more readily into spaces between irregular flagstones than into the narrow gaps between bricks and pavers. Wherever possible, choose the most pervious option in order to allow water to soak in more readily. In certain cases, however, you'll want a solid surface. If you've ever seen a gravel path wash out in a downpour, for instance, you know that sometimes water flows too quickly and too heavily to be absorbed. Gushing across

Designer Lori Daul extended a ground-level covered porch with a decomposed granite and concrete paver patio.

the water-saving garden

gravel or unmortared stone, torrents of water during a heavy thunderstorm can scour out gravel and the sand between flagstones, necessitating time-consuming repairs. Concrete, or even closely set pavers, can withstand such tests and may be the right choice, especially near downspouts or at the bottom of a hill. With impervious paving, shift your focus to slowing and retaining the water that flows off of it.

add pavilions, play spaces, ponds, and other fun features

The appeal of a lawn can't hold a candle to the many fun features you can add to your garden that will entice you and your family outdoors while requiring much less water, or no water at all. From a pavilion or gazebo that offers a shady spot to enjoy a garden view to a washer pit or bocce court for family-friendly games to a labyrinth for contemplative strolls to a simple container pond filled with water lilies and goldfish, fun features give you a reason to step outside and hang out for a while. After all, if you have outdoor space, why not enjoy it? Think about what you and your family might enjoy most—ask their opinion; you want them to be invested in it too—and carve out lawn to make room.

Less lawn generally means less water use, even if you choose a water feature to replace it. Just be sure, if you live in a hot or dry climate, to opt for a water feature that isn't wasteful, like a reflective still pond in part shade rather than a splashing fountain in full sun, which can require more-frequent refills due to wind and evaporation. While it may seem counterintuitive to have a water feature in a water-saving garden, a pond loses much less water to evaporation than is typically used to irrigate a lawn of the same size, especially if sited in afternoon shade. In a dry climate a vessel of water can be viewed, as landscape architect Christine Ten Eyck has said, as a sacred element, all the more precious for representing a rare resource. Treat it as such. Dig out a shallow circular pool (geometric ponds are easier to pull off than naturalistic shapes) or, even simpler, make a container pond out of a galvanized-steel stock tank. Then surround it with permeable paving like gravel or unmortared stone for easy viewing and tending. Such a pond makes a beautiful focal point for the garden and may become its spiritual heart.

Anchoring a low-water garden, a stock-tank container pond is a wildlife-attracting focal point.

Families with children may opt for a play space of some kind. Swing sets and forts situated within a generous fall zone of cushioning pea gravel or wood mulch (12 inches deep is ideal; remove the lawn and install the play structure on bare, level ground, and then add the cushioning mulch or gravel) can take up a lot of space formerly devoted to lawn, and children often prefer such hideaways and climbing structures to the bare openness of grass. Unless your child regularly plays a ball sport at home (in these days of organized sports, municipal fields get more use than home lawns), he or she will likely prefer the delights of smooth garden paths disappearing around the bend for tricycling or scootering, a big sandbox for digging, or a tree for climbing. Hidden spaces partially screened by shrubs or grasses are particularly appealing to young children. A simple bamboo-pole tepee shrouded with vines can also make a delightful hideaway; just lean tall bamboo poles together in a tepee shape, secure with wire or twine at the top, and have your child help you plant seeds of annual vines or beans around the base. One of the best play spaces my children ever encountered contained a random assortment of small boulders, on which they loved to climb. In a child's imagination, these may transform into an armada of spaceships, islands of safety in a shark-finned sea, or castle towers. Site your play space near a shady tree and spread cushioning mulch around it, and you'll have eliminated a good deal of lawn and given your children a reason to run outside to play every day. Older kids and adults like to play too, of course, and outdoor games can be great for entertaining. Although installation can be expensive, bocce courts are currently in vogue. Alternatively, a do-it-yourselfer can easily and thriftily install a horseshoe or washer pit for plenty of family fun.

If you're more of a lie-in-a-hammock type and would enjoy a garden retreat, site a shade pavilion, ramada, hammock, or garden swing away from the house, with an inviting path leading out to it. Lay a carpet of mulch or gravel to keep the area for relaxing, not mowing and watering. Gathering spaces like fire pits surrounded by casual seating—think Adirondack chairs, metal motel chairs, or even bench-sized boulders—offer convivial relaxation for family and friends. It's a primal delight to sit around a fire, gazing into the flames and feeling the heat push away the chill. You can make your own fire pit by excavating several inches of soil and building a low, stacked-stone wall around the pit or simply using an old metal tractor-tire rim to contain the fire (try Craigslist). If wood smoke exacerbates respiratory problems, or if wood fires are illegal in your community due to fire risk or smoke pollution, choose a gas fire table instead. You'll need to have it hooked up to a natural gas line from your home or purchase a unit fueled by propane tank. For safety, site your fire pit away from overhanging trees, and pave the space with gravel or flagstones rather than flammable wood mulch or pine straw.

A bocce court is multifunctional for young families, offering space to play with toy cars, toss or kick a ball, and even dance, according to homeowner Andrea Testa-Vought.

put side yards to work

Side yards are often narrow, shady, and rarely used, and trying to maintain lawn there is a waste of water and effort. Instead, think of ways to put your side yards, which offer especially valuable space on small properties, to work. If you have a fenced back yard and gates on one or both sides, connect front-yard paving to side-yard paths, thereby eliminating more lawn and creating an invitation to explore the back garden. Add a welcoming arbor at the gate and paint both of them an accent color to attract the eye and let visitors know there is more to see in back. This is especially effective if you plant a pretty side-yard garden that comes into view when you open the gate. You'll get double the pleasure from a side garden if the space is viewable through interior windows. Dress it up with a handsome path and a focal-point feature you can enjoy from indoors, like a burbling fountain to attract birds, an interesting sculpture, or even a tiny patio with room for a couple of colorful chairs. Grow vines on your fence or a freestanding trellis and add evergreen shrubs and groundcovers to create a view you'll enjoy indoors and out.

Corral trash bins so they don't become an unwelcome focal point of your side garden.

If the side yard is not on view from interior windows, you might prefer to use it as a work and storage space. To gain more storage in a fenced side yard, extend your fence forward, toward the front corner of your house, but not all the way to the corner. Leave at least a foot of space between the corner of the house and the connecting fence and gate. This gives the house depth from the street and avoids a flat, two-dimensional appearance where house and fence meet. In the enclosed space, set up a potting bench and bin storage for gardening supplies. Trash and recycling bins can also be neatly stored here, hidden from view and easily rolled out on your front path. If you lack a fence for hiding such workaday items, build a simple wooden screen—framed horizontal laths or premade lattice work well—about 5 feet tall, wide enough to hide your bins but leaving room to walk around it, and attach

it to the side of your house. Stain or paint the screen to dress it up, have it blend in, or add a pop of color, as you wish. Floor the entire side yard with gravel or pavers to make this space completely functional without requiring any watering at all.

Low-water plants help keep a side garden low-maintenance.

grow native—but enjoy well-adapted plants too

Not all that long ago, native plants got little respect, scorned as mere weeds and brush that needed clearing before garden making could occur.

Ahead-of-their-time native-plant enthusiasts faced resistance from neighbors concerned about an unkempt look. Municipal grass-mowing codes were enforced against them. Even if you did want to grow native plants, you couldn't find them at your local nursery. Over the past few decades, however, gardening with native plants has achieved not just acceptance but mainstream popularity, especially in the western United States, where sparse rainfall and watering restrictions have made it clear that gardens full of thirsty exotics are unsustainable. Native plants are frequently sold in independent nurseries or online, and plenty of books about growing them have been written. Most botanical gardens now feature native-plant gardens amid their other offerings. Planted entirely with native plants, the Lady Bird Johnson Wildflower Center in Austin, Texas, is also dedicated to research and education about them.

Native plants impart a sense of place to a garden. While you'd have a hard time distinguishing between pictures of homogeneous lawns in Indiana, Georgia, and Colorado, a garden with native plants creates local flavor.

Salvia greggii attracts a hummingbird.

Aha! you'd say: that's an Oklahoma garden, or that one looks like Connecticut. You feel a connection to your home region, and to the natural landscape around you, when you cultivate plants that can be seen growing wild along hiking trails or in greenbelts. (Don't remove them from the wild, though—that is an illegal practice that harms delicate ecosystems. Instead, buy from reputable sources and native plant society sales or collect a few seeds and propagate your own plants.)

Natives also provide what indigenous wildlife requires for food or habitat.

Having evolved side by side, they uniquely meet each other's needs, whether for sustenance and larval habitat or for pollination and seed dispersal. Watching beneficial creatures like bees, butterflies, birds, praying mantises, and ladybugs appear in your garden to nectar, feed, build nests, lay eggs, and raise young is one of the most gratifying reasons to make a garden, creating a natural balance that you never see in a yard with an empty lawn. Gardens that appeal to wildlife, with a water source (like a birdbath) and native plants to shelter and feed them, act as way stations and wildlife corridors in our paved-over cities and suburbs. Every person who plants a garden for wildlife contributes to this network of safe zones.

Despite our current love affair with native plants, defining "native" has proven to be a slippery business. Some say *native* means "growing here (in the United States) before European settlement" or "growing in a certain geographical area" (the size of which is up for debate). I tend not to be too picky about it myself, accepting as native any plant that has evolved to occur naturally in a particular local or regional ecosystem. However you define them, native plants are naturally well suited to their native climate and can be self-sufficient in a garden, provided you meet their innate preferences for shade or sun, dry or moist soil, and so on. Be wary of plant labels that advertise "native plant" without specifying where they're native to or the conditions they need. Even across a city, much less a state, soil types and elevation can vary widely, making a plant suitable for one side of town but not the other. Native plants, like all plants, need to be planted in the conditions they prefer. To learn which natives are best suited to your particular conditions, shop at nurseries that specialize in natives and read their plant labels carefully. Also, ask your local extension office if they have lists of appropriate native plants. Attend native-plant sales in your area and don't be shy about asking questions about the plants offered there.

I must dispel one more illusion about natives: they are not, by definition, drought tolerant, although they're often praised for that quality. The fact is, a native plant may be thirsty or water thrifty, sun loving or shade loving, and anything in between. After all, every plant is native to some place. The key is to choose plants native to the specific conditions of your garden.

Clockwise from top left: Eryngium and aster, two drought-tolerant plants for late-summer color.

A garden composed largely of plants native to the desert Southwest looks at home there.

Native pollinator plants on display at a plant sale.

A native plant garden in New York has a temperate-climate lushness.

A formally designed native plant garden shows that natives work even in traditional settings.

Well-chosen natives are likely to survive the vicissitudes of your climate because they'll have evolved to live in it. They should be able to thrive on normal levels of rainfall, with supplemental watering during dry periods to keep them looking garden worthy. Remember, no plant is drought proof; all plants need water. But plants that have evolved to grow in a particular region are better equipped to survive the natural cycles of rainfall and drought.

One aspect of growing native plants continues to lag: how to design with natives. Readily embraced in naturalistic or wildscaped gardens, native plants are less commonly used in more structured designs, whether traditionally formal, clean-lined contemporary, or simply HOA friendly. Can natives, in fact, be used effectively in nonnaturalistic gardens? You bet. After all, plants are plants, as far as design goes. When designing with natives, keep in mind that you can use them just as you do exotic plants, whether for foundation shrubs, topiary, allées, block-planting a single species, or just blending in with the neighbors' traditional landscaping. Here are some tips:

* **Replace like with like.** Choose a native species with a form similar to the traditional plant for which you'd like a locally suitable substitute—for example, dwarf yaupon holly (*Ilex vomitoria* 'Nana'), which has a naturally rounded form and a dense leaf structure, in lieu of clipped boxwood (*Buxus* spp.). A native plant that grows in the same way and to a similar height may make the perfect substitute for an overused, water-needy exotic.

* **Vary foliage size.** In arid and semi-arid climates, native plants tend to have tiny leaves that help stave off water loss. A garden full of such fine texture can easily become a blur of undifferentiated foliage. Break up that sea of fine texture with broad-leaved or structural plants like agave, yucca, spineless prickly pear, and ocotillo, or whatever strong forms are available in your climate. Don't worry—it won't make your garden look like a desert to have a few spiny plants in it. Provided they have good drainage and are grown with other drought-tolerant, sun-loving plants, they mingle quite nicely with flowering perennials and ornamental trees.

* **Add structure with hardscape.** Defy the popular conception of native gardens as messy by adding strong architectural features: defined paths, low walls, seating areas, and other space-defining hardscape. I don't mean that you have to spend big bucks on fancy stone terraces or walls (although those are lovely if you have the means). Defined gravel paths and neatly edged patios work well too and are less expensive and easy to install yourself. And anyone can build a low retaining wall to create an elevation change that adds interest and definition to the garden.

* **Choose native plants with a long season of interest.** The non-native plants so often used in gardens across the country are popular for a reason: they are sturdy, long-lasting performers. Of course they may also be water guzzlers and intolerant of hot, dry summers, so when you turn to native substitutes, look for those that put on a good show for more than just a few glorious weeks.

Look beyond flowers when choosing plants. Foliage gives long-lasting impact, so choose native plants for leaf color and overall form rather than for fleeting flowers.

* **Think about focal points.** This is a traditional design technique, and it works just as well in a native garden—maybe better because it adds essential structure—to direct the eye toward certain features or indicate where one should walk. Plant an allée of native trees, drawing the eye inevitably toward a focal-point garden ornament. Or plant a large pot with a native plant and place it midway along a path so as to attract the eye and encourage visitors to stop and look.

* **Regular grooming matters.** Remember that native plants, just like traditional exotics, require maintenance to look their best. Natives have been sold so well to the public as bulletproof drought survivors that people often think you can just plant them and walk away. Not only do native plants require regular water to get established, just as nonnatives do, but they also look better in a garden setting with regular grooming. Have you ever gone hiking locally and really looked at the wild landscape? Is that what you want your garden to look like? I'm not saying a wildscape is bad. I'm just saying that's not what most people want in front of their houses, especially in traditional neighborhoods. Rather than let your natives grow wild in your garden, take time to prune them as necessary. I don't mean shearing them into meatballs, mind you, just cutting back dead stems and branches, pruning for shape, pulling up or moving seedlings that are taking over your gravel paths, and giving your garden a cared-for look. Such maintenance is made easier from the start by choosing plants based on their mature sizes, so that you don't have to continually prune over-grown foundation shrubs or trees that outgrew their placement.

Because native plants can reduce your garden's watering needs, are beneficial to wildlife, and give your garden a sense of place, it's easy to fall in love with them to the exclusion of exotics. Certainly if you want to make an all-native garden, you should go for it. But since gardening is also about play and experimentation and, let's face it, plant lust, I urge you not to feel guilty about growing well-adapted nonnatives too. By well-adapted nonnatives I mean plants that aren't naturally found in a particular locale but that hail from similar climates and soils elsewhere, thereby assuring that they'll be tough survivors in your garden. For example, in coastal California, where summers are dry, winters are wet, and temperatures are mild, you could try plants from the Mediterranean Sea basin, South Africa, coastal Australia, and coastal Chile—all commonly described as Mediterranean climates. In the humid subtropical Southeast, plants from warm, temperate regions in China and Japan tend to grow well.

And you need not apologize for growing common, well-adapted nonnatives. They may not be exciting choices, but they don't deserve to be shunned just for being successful. Take antique roses, for example. Some varieties can thrive in a multitude of climates and have been shared all over the world because of their hardiness. If you love them and they don't require more water than your other plants, why not add a few to your garden? In concert with native plants, well-adapted exotics can satisfy the longing of a plant collector and add diversity to your garden. Just be sure to choose well-adapted exotics rather than hothouse beauties that will chain you to the hose. And research any plant you're considering to make sure it's not invasive in your climate. Sometimes being well adapted is a scary quality in a plant that just doesn't know when to stop and that outcompetes other plants through rampant growth or seeds out with abandon into the wild. You can find invasive plant lists for your region online. Check before you buy or accept a passed-along plant from a friend.

Drought-tolerant rose of Sharon (*Althaea* spp.) is commonly grown throughout the southern and Midwestern United States, although it's native to Asia.

ripple-zone planting and rethinking lush

By the time you've decided on your garden's layout
and installed paths, patios, fun features, and other
hardscape, you'll be craving some greenery. It's time
to plant!

But before you dash to the garden center to load up your cart, you'll need
to do some planning to make sure your garden helps you save water instead
of waste it. Here's a simple visualization exercise to guide you in what to
plant where.

Imagine your house as a stone dropped into a pond, and your garden as
a series of ever-widening ripples moving out from the house. Each of the
ripples represents a thirst zone—that is, a threshold of water needs for the
plants within it. Plants with compatible water needs should be planted
alongside each other in each zone. Plant your thirstiest plants within the
smallest ripple, closest to the house and the garden hose, where you can
easily give them the extra attention they need and also appreciate them
on a daily basis; after all, why choose a plant that demands coddling with
extra water unless it's something you really love? In each ripple extending
outward from the house, choose increasingly drought-tolerant plants. If
your yard is very large, the farthest ripple may be a nonirrigated natural area
planted (if at all; you could just let it be wild) with natives and well-adapted

Columbine, which likes
a little extra water in
hot climates, is enjoyed
close to the house.

Ferns and a bubbling water feature are sited near the house for easier tending.

species that can survive on rainfall alone. This ripple-zone planting strategy helps you to group plants according to similar watering needs, which makes less work for you, is better for the health of the plants, makes irrigating more efficient, and reduces overall watering.

Of course this is a visualization tactic, not a hard-and-fast rule. You may have areas of damp shade at the far end of your garden that call for moisture-loving plants. Or perhaps your garden along the front porch is blasted by sun and reflected heat from the driveway, and drought-tolerant species would do well there. Respond to any special conditions in your garden by planting appropriately, since matching the right plant to the right spot is key to a garden's success. But all else being equal, planting and grouping according to thirst zones makes good sense and saves water.

Let's start with the inner zone, closest to the house. Here you might wish to indulge in plants that, although they have higher water needs, you find especially exciting or are meaningful to you in some way. Maybe your grandfather grew ferns, and they remind you of him. Maybe you love surrounding your patio with the bold, luxuriant leaves of tropicals each summer. Or perhaps you crave a container pond in order to grow water lilies and attract birds and other wildlife. This is the place to do it. But be as selective as you can. Remember, the inner, highest-thirst zone is also, to save water, the smallest, and your plant choices should reflect that. The nice thing is that, being close to the house, the plants in this zone will be under your nose on a daily basis, whether you pass them getting into the car or admire them through your living-room window, making them all the more enjoyable. Their proximity will also help you to stay on top of the watering. The second ripple zone is for plants that prefer drier conditions. Maybe they can get by with weekly irrigation in summer and need no supplemental water in wetter seasons. A third ripple zone might contain plants that need a deep watering only once a month. The outer zone might be left nonirrigated and largely wild, with perhaps occasional trimming for neatness. This is especially appropriate for large gardens that abut a greenbelt, meadow, or other wild area, and it will help the garden blend into the natural landscape.

Along a path leading away from the house to a wild canyon, tough natives require less attention.

If you're installing an automatic irrigation system, have the zones programmed according to the water needs in each ripple zone so that your plants receive the amount of water that's right for them and no more. The inner zone will need to run longer or more often than the outer zones, and the farthest zone should be watered least often (an occasional deep watering is generally better for drought-tolerant plants than frequent, shallow waterings) or not at all. If you're watering via soaker hose or hose-end sprinkler, set a timer when you turn it on so that you don't overwater the outer zones. Remember, if you give everything the same amount of water, you're using more water than you need to and you've wasted the time you took in planting your garden by each plant's watering need. Your plants will be happier if given the right amount of water, and you'll be much happier with your water bill.

Left: In a waterwise desert garden, open spaces between plants reduce competition for water.

Right: In a rainy-climate garden, tight spacing crowds out weeds.

One last reminder: When planting your ripple zones, don't forget to pay attention to sun and shade, and group plants by those conditions as well. Even if a group of different plants likes dry soil, they won't be happy together if some crave sun and others shade.

Ripple-zone planting can be applied to any garden in any climate where irrigation is used in order to save water. But there's another factor to consider, and it depends entirely on your climate—or rather, it depends on the relative aridity or humidity of your local climate. I call it the lush factor. In late spring or early summer, search out wild places and undeveloped lots in your area. What do you see? Forest with lots of leafy undergrowth? Meadows filled with grasses and a few trees? Does a dense growth of plants conceal undisturbed soil? If so, you likely live in a humid climate with regular rainfall for at least part of the year. Or do you see sparse grasses or scrubby shrubs with bare ground between them? Are there few trees, and if so, are they found mainly near dry creeks or washes? Is the soil exposed and gravelly, and is the ground hard even after a rain? If so, you likely live in an arid or semi-arid climate with scant rain or long periods of drought between monsoon seasons. Whatever your wild spaces show you—dense, bushy growth or an open landscape of individual plants—there's a reason why plants grow close together or at arm's length, and it's based on available water. Plants that don't need to compete as much for water tend to grow densely. Those that must put up a scrappy fight for every sip grow farther apart. To plant appropriately for your climate and save water, emulate natural patterns in your garden. Use Mother Nature's spacing as a guideline.

Of course, a garden is not wild, and few of us want gardens that look that way, especially in suburban and urban neighborhoods. Those in arid climates might prefer a more lush landscape than would ever occur naturally. That's okay; there's wiggle room. Just keep the lush factor in mind as you plan what to plant, especially if you live in a dry or summer-dry part of the country. Whereas gardens in rainy regions benefit from dense spacing—which crowds out weeds and covers bare soil, giving weed seeds no room to germinate—gardens in arid regions benefit from incorporating "breathing room" around plants, from several feet to several yards, depending on how much rain is available to support them. With less competition for water, widely spaced plants are better able to thrive in extreme heat and dry conditions.

Dry-climate plants need space to grow spreading roots that seek out moisture.

Don't try to replicate those lush and leafy temperate-climate gardens shown in so many gardening magazines. Your bold, open landscape demands a garden to match. Spacing your plants farther apart gives them room to grow a spreading root system that can soak up the rain when it finally comes. Even if you're willing to irrigate from time to time, striving for a garden that largely gets by on natural rainfall is a big help in saving water.

timing is everything: when to plant

Intoxicated by the first balmy breezes and earthy scents of spring, otherwise reasonable people suddenly turn into gardening zombies, lurching toward the nearest nursery with arms outstretched, hoarsely shouting, "Plaaaants!"

They fill carts with flowering annuals, perennials, and shrubs, fingers twitching with desire to dig in the soil and brighten their gardens. Does this sound like anyone you know?

Springtime's reprieve from winter's gloom has the power to entice the least impulsive gardener into the nursery aisles. However, while we may yearn to put shovel to soil as the days grow longer and warmer, spring is actually eclipsed by autumn as the best planting season for anyone trying to save water. Ironically, come autumn, many gardeners (particularly those in cold-winter climates) are prepping their gardens for the first freeze—draining irrigation systems, cleaning and putting away tools, and covering patio furniture—and not thinking about planting. Even in mild-winter regions people commonly overlook fall as a great planting season.

Fall actually offers significant advantages over spring for establishing new plants with less water, including warm soil, moderate air temperature,

By shopping in autumn, you'll find plants that offer late-season interest to your garden.

and the reappearance of rainfall in dry-summer climates. The mellowness of fall, in which summer's heat has waned but warmth lingers in the soil, means new plants have an easier time growing the root system they need to get established. In mild-winter climates, where the ground never freezes, plants that are planted in fall continue to grow their roots all winter, even as top growth dies back during freezes. Autumn rains help too by providing some of the moisture all new plants require until their roots become water-seeking support systems. By the time spring rolls around, fall-planted plants have developed a solid root system that allows them to put more energy into growing foliage and will help them survive the hot summer. Contrast this scenario with a spring planting. In spring the soil is still cool, awakening gradually from winter's chill. Cool soil inhibits the root growth new plants depend on to become self-sufficient. By the time the soil has warmed up, temperatures above ground are growing hotter and sunlight more intense, stressing new plants and increasing their watering needs. You'll end up having to water more often to keep new plants alive that first summer if you plant in spring rather than fall, and this is doubly true for gardeners in hot, dry-summer climates.

Left: Colorful spring annuals—a magnet for winter-weary gardeners

Right: Shop for shrubs and trees in fall since they benefit most from autumn planting.

Even if you live where the ground freezes in winter, fall is still a good time to plant. Just be sure to start early enough to get new plants settled in before the soil freezes, and water your new plants all the way through fall. If you drain your irrigation system well before first freeze, you'll need to commit to hand watering your new plants, which, lacking an established root system, are not able to search out water in the soil.

Because of their larger size and higher initial watering needs, shrubs and trees are ideally suited to planting in fall—and in winter, too, in places where the ground doesn't freeze. To grow their substantial root systems, they benefit the most from extra months of root-growing time, while top growth is dormant. But even most perennials can be planted in the cooler and (in some regions) rainier months so they can grow their roots all winter, or until the soil freezes, and be better prepared for summer. Again, be sure to water thoroughly at planting and keep root balls moist throughout the fall until (if) the ground freezes. New plants, even drought-tolerant and native plants, need regular water the first year to get established. Even so, you'll still save on watering next summer by planting in fall.

Of course there are exceptions, and certain plants should be planted only in spring unless you live in a frost-free climate. Frost-tender plants like some succulents and cacti, subtropical perennials and warm-season growers like bamboo, and any plant for which you're pushing your zone—that is, trying to grow a plant considered marginally cold-hardy in your region—should be planted in the spring, after all risk of freezing weather is past. Read the label or check online to learn whether a plant is solidly winter-hardy in your region before planting in the fall. You'll often find tender plants on discount in the fall, as nurseries try to clear out their stock, but don't be tempted unless you have a greenhouse in which to store them for the winter. Such plants need warm weather to grow, and they respond poorly to freezes if not well established. If planted in spring and established over the summer, they'll have a much better chance of surviving their first winter.

To save water, avoid planting almost everything in summer, when heat and/or lack of rain puts extra stress on plants before they've had time to grow a supportive root system. Exceptions include desert plants like cacti, agaves,

the water-saving garden

yuccas, and other extremely heat-tolerant and dry-adapted plants. If you must plant in summer, plant early in the morning, water well, and set up shade cloth or even a lawn chair over the new plant to shield it from the sun's rays. A plant "parasol" can be a lifesaver for a plant that's just left the pampered conditions of a nursery and moved into the glare of the summer sun in your garden. Leave the filtered shade in place for a week and keep the plant well watered to reduce transplant shock.

Even the most well-intentioned, fall-planting gardener can't plant what isn't available, however. While you can often find great deals at nurseries in the fall, especially in colder climates where garden centers shut down for the winter, the selection may be slimmer than what you'd find in spring or summer. Nurseries sell what looks good at the moment. Although you may find beautiful, fall-blooming grasses and perennials or plants with autumn color or winter berries, a hunt for spring or early summer bloomers may prove fruitless. In that case, buy what you can when it's available, starting with all the plants you can locate in the fall. When you plant them, leave space for the plants you want but can't find for sale in the fall. Then, in the spring, you can fill in the gaps once fresh nursery stock is available. Just remember that your fall-planted plants will be more established than your spring-planted ones, and you'll need to baby the new ones accordingly.

Opposite, clockwise from top left: Nurseries generally have a good stock of trees, shrubs, and perennials for fall planting. In cold-winter climates, check end-of-summer sales.

Fall blooms like amaranth offer late season nectar stops for butterflies.

Ornamental grasses bloom alongside roses and cuphea in autumn.

Fall is a great time to plant native perennials.

This page: Desert plants are best planted in late spring, after last frost, or in summer.

hot pots: saving water in container and balcony gardens

If you don't have access to a yard because you live in an apartment or condo, you can still create a beautiful garden through the use of containers.

Container gardens bring greenery and life to patios, decks, balconies, and rooftops that otherwise may lack a physical connection to the earth, creating inviting views inside and out and providing rest stops for wildlife. Despite the pleasure they bring to space-challenged gardeners, container plants tend to be water hogs—and no wonder. With roots constricted in a relatively small amount of soil, and lacking the warmth, moisture, and insulation of ground soil, potted plants may also contend with a slew of inhospitable conditions: incessant wind, reflected heat, long hours of intense sunlight or deep shade, and exposure to temperature extremes. Endless watering may appear to be the price one must pay to keep a container garden alive. For those without access to an outdoor spigot, this involves frequent lugging of heavy buckets or watering cans from the kitchen sink or bathtub. With some relatively easy changes, however, container gardeners can reap the rewards of saving water, including lower water bills, less maintenance, and the satisfaction of conserving our most essential resource.

Ice plant (*Delosperma* sp.) needs little water for spectacular flowering.

Let's start with the kinds of containers you use. First of all, go big. Forget using dainty little pots outdoors; save them for your kitchen windowsill. Small pots can hold only a few cups of potting soil, which dries out quickly when exposed to reflected heat and drying winds. Instead, choose large pots and oversized containers like half-barrels and stock tanks. (If weight is a concern, as on a balcony or rooftop, see the additional suggestions that follow.) Large pots give plants more room to grow a strong, anchoring root system, and more soil provides a greater capacity for holding moisture and better insulation against drying wind, cold snaps, and baking sun.

The type of pot matters also. Opt for ceramic pots with a shiny, hard-fired glaze or containers made of cast stone, lightweight metal, wood, fiberglass, or plastic. These materials are either waterproof or insulating, thereby helping the soil inside stay moist. Steer clear of terracotta pots. While terracotta is affordable and classic in style, its porosity allows soil to dry out quickly, and it may crack in freezing weather. If you already have large terracotta pots on hand, try lining them with heavy plastic to reduce water loss, remembering to poke a few holes in the bottom for drainage. As for metal containers like stock tanks and galvanized steel boxes, gardeners sometimes worry that the metal will heat up in summer and transfer damaging heat to the roots of plants. While this may be a concern when using small metal pots in hot climates, plants in larger containers don't seem to suffer. I've planted many a large stock tank in Austin, Texas, where summer days routinely heat up to the upper 90 degrees Fahrenheit and warm nights offer little relief, and I've never noticed any problems with plants getting steamed. Choosing tough, heat-tolerant plants, which is a good waterwise practice anyway, should ensure that any minor heat transference in the soil isn't a concern. Whichever type of pot you choose, make sure it has several holes or at least one large hole for drainage. An inability to drain freely can quickly kill a potted plant, the roots of which essentially suffocate. You can help with drainage by raising containers off the floor, using pot feet or a few bricks, and by taking care not to block the drain holes. Avoid using saucers under pots: if they don't evaporate quickly, they obstruct drainage and give mosquitoes a place to breed.

Left: Choose large pots, which don't dry out as quickly as smaller containers.

Below left: An overscaled red pot makes a fun focal point and needs less frequent watering.

Below right: Large planters need not be pricey. Even old dustbins can be pressed into service if you punch a few drainage holes in the bottom.

A mix of glazed pottery and galvanized buckets creates an eye-catching display.

On a rooftop, balcony, or deck, where the combined weight of people, furnishings, and containers filled with wet soil is a concern, you should follow your building management's rules and weight limits and consult a structural engineer before starting an extensive container garden. Choose lightweight materials to reduce the weight load. You can still use large pots, but opt for those made of lightweight materials like plastic, fiberglass, wood, and thin sheets of steel. To avoid the weight (and expense) of completely filling an especially large container with potting soil, layer the bottom one-third with a light, long-lasting material like crumpled plastic milk jugs. This is fine for small, shallow-rooted plants like succulents and most edibles, but for larger plants, you may need to fill the pot with soil in order to give roots room to grow. You can also use lightweight potting soil to reduce the weight load, although keep in mind that such potting soils and soilless mixes will dry out faster than regular potting soil. Using dry-adapted plants will help you avoid incessant watering.

Reducing weight is critical when making a garden in the sky, but the resulting lightweight pots are vulnerable to wind damage. Gusts of wind can be strong several stories above ground, or even on an elevated deck, causing furniture to overturn, umbrellas to fly away, and potted plants to blow over. Wind also presents a serious danger to people below if it causes potted plants or other items to blow over the railing. Having ensured that

Metal and glazed ceramic planters mingle in a contemporary patio garden.

your large pots are not too heavy for balcony or rooftop use, you'll want to make certain they stay put. Try wrapping strong but unobtrusive wire around your pots and attaching them to well-anchored railings for added stability, assuming that your HOA or lease agreement doesn't forbid it. Wind strips moisture from plants' leaves and from the top layer of soil, drying them out and increasing their watering needs. The constant buffeting and noise of a strong wind can make it unpleasant to spend time outdoors, especially if you're trying to read or eat. Plant placement can help. Cluster your biggest pots and taller plants along the rail to help break up and redirect gusts of wind, sheltering more-delicate plants and seating areas. Tall grasses, coastal plants (which have evolved to be wind tolerant), and even squat shrubs can make good windbreaks. You can also make a windscreen by securing a piece of clear Plexiglass or a sturdy slatted screen to the windward side of your railing. It need only be as tall as the railing to offer protection, and it'll be less obtrusive and easier to secure if kept at rail height.

Shade also helps keep containers moist. Cluster pots together, and position taller plants and those with cascading leaves, like ornamental grasses, so that they provide filtered shade for other potted plants. You can also grow a potted vine along your deck or balcony railing, creating a green screen to shade your other container plants. Air circulation is important too. Just as sun-heated concrete sizzles your bare feet, so do potted plants

the water-saving garden

"feel the burn" when placed on baking-hot surfaces. Use three or four pot feet—L-shaped or decorative wedges typically made of terracotta or glazed pottery—to lift each container about an inch off the ground, allowing air to flow under the pot and water to drain properly. Your pots will stay moist longer, and your flooring will be protected from water stains.

As important as pot type, shade, and wind protection (but much more fun!) is plant choice. Container plants should be selected not just for beauty but for drought tolerance, wind tolerance, and general hardiness. Think of your plants as astronaut-explorers, boldly going where no plant has gone before. To thrive in an alien environment, separated from the earth, yet without need of constant watering, they must be tough and adaptable, not prima donnas. Making smart planting choices will help you reduce your watering chore over the long term, so research your options, keeping in mind that container gardens, especially elevated ones, tend to be hotter in summer, colder in winter, and dry year round. Unless your balcony or patio is quite shady and protected from wind, avoid lush, large-leaved plants, especially in hot climates, because they tend to need a lot more water. Opt for dry-loving native and adapted plants that won't wilt at the first hint of summer. Also, small, dry-adapted shrubs like dwarf bottlebrush and herbs like rosemary are water thrifty, and such plants are often tolerant of wind as well. If you live in a mild-winter climate or are willing to bring large potted plants indoors in winter (putting your pots on casters makes this easier), try growing succulents and cacti, which store water in their leaves or stems, making them very drought tolerant. Such plants are handsome in containers, combining the bold architecture of their form with interesting foliage textures and colors. In colder climates you might choose to grow tender succulents as annuals, enjoying them from spring through fall until the first freeze. It's not any different than buying flowering annuals every spring, and succulents will need far less water. They do grow more slowly, however, so pack them tightly into your pots rather than buying just a few plants

Opposite: Clustering potted plants together helps shield potting soil from the sun and wind.

Below: A tall ornamental grass shelters smaller potted plants.

and hoping they'll fill in. In winter, you can still enjoy your containers by filling them with pretty branches or grapevine balls wrapped with outdoor twinkle lights for a festive winter glow.

It's fashionable these days, and simpler, to use one plant per container, arranging plants at different heights through the use of taller and shorter containers or by elevating a few pots on stacked pavers. However, you may prefer to combine multiple plants in your large containers, which can result in striking and artistic combinations. Just make sure that each plant's water and sun or shade needs are the same if they're grouped in one pot. They need to be good bedfellows if they're going to share tight quarters. Also, when planting succulents and cacti, use sharp-draining potting soil mixed with chicken grit or perlite to prevent rot; for other dry-adapted plants, lightweight potting soil will keep containers light and provide good drainage. After planting, layer 1 to 2 inches of mulch atop the potting soil to keep dirt from splattering when it rains or when you water and to keep plant roots cool and moist. Good options include washed pea gravel, colored glass beads, seashells, or shredded hardwood mulch.

Succulents and cacti don't need a lot of water, even in containers. However, many need to be protected from winter freezes.

Once your containers are planted and mulched, you'll need to water them regularly, more often at first, to establish your plants and then ease off gradually to see how long you can push it between waterings. Watering frequency, even with the water-saving tips outlined here, will depend on your specific conditions and on the plants you chose. It's quite easy to overwater succulents and cacti, although if planted in sharp-draining soil in pots with good drainage, they won't mind extra water in the summer; in winter you probably won't need to water them at all, as they prefer to be dry during cool weather. In general, for all your potted plants, water early in the morning, and water until it runs out of the bottom of the pot to flush any salt buildup from the soil. To get the most out of the water you use, place potted plants under any hanging containers to catch the overflow. And when possible, use collected rainwater or recycle household water to water

One plant per pot shows off each plant's form.

your containers. You can collect a good deal of clean, nonsoapy water by simply putting a bucket under your showerhead while waiting for the water to run warm, and you can carry this straight to the balcony or patio to water your pots. If you travel a lot or tend to forget to water, and if you have an outdoor faucet, you might wish to install a drip system for your pots and put it on a timer. Drip irrigation is as efficient for watering containers as it is for in-ground plants. Just keep in mind that the timer should be adjusted depending on time of year; plants need more water in summer than in winter. Don't just set it and forget it, or you'll end up using more water than you need.

Planted green-roof systems also bring life and beauty to rooftop gardens, and they help reduce runoff as well. However, because of weight load and other structural and safety concerns, they're beyond the scope of water-saving methods detailed in this book. See recommended resources for further information.

Large pots planted with drought-tolerant natives brighten the edge of a patio.

part four

oasis or mirage?
creating the ILLUSION of
water in the garden

the water feature as a symbol of abundance

Unfortunately, it can take a drought to make us really appreciate water. Experience a few bone-dry months creeping by, and a sudden rain shower will elicit giddy relief, a deep sense of gratitude, and a fervent resolution never to take water for granted again.

If you live in a region that experiences frequent droughts, cycles of drought and flood, or dry months broken by monsoon rains, then you already know what it is to wait for rains that turn the land green again. More of us will be experiencing this in the future. Climate change is expected to cause more-frequent and longer droughts in regions that are already dry, and in wetter regions, periods of unusual dryness between rains. Everywhere, assumptions about normal rainfall patterns are being challenged, and cities are planning for drought or storm management—or both.

Amid all this climatic uncertainty, one fact remains constant: water is life. Without this most sacred element, neither gardens nor we ourselves could live. Because of its scarcity, nowhere is water more revered than in the desert, where, since ancient times, people have built protectively walled, inward-focused gardens around a symbolic display of water. In the influential Persian garden tradition, a central water feature—typically a narrow rill bisected by another, or a long reflecting pool with a simple

A fountain with a hidden basin recirculates water, creating the illusion of an endless supply.

A simple container pond in a steel bowl holds a water lily.

line of trees for shade on either side—represented paradise on earth, with waters that would never run dry. As the style evolved in semi-arid southern Spain, the Moors built courtyards around a central pool or burbling fountain to cool the air, with fruit trees and herbs along the edges to soften the space and provide food. Eventually Spanish colonizers exported the style to the New World, where it translated well to the hot, dry desert Southwest.

In our water-saving gardens today, even in those that aren't made in the Spanish courtyard style, we can draw inspiration from the idea of a desert oasis. No matter where you live, whether challenged by drought or blessed with abundant rain, making a water-saving garden is about respecting the value of water. It's about using water judiciously and thriftily, and honoring the place you live by creating a garden that belongs there. In such gardens, water is vested with symbolic power. You needn't shy away from small extravagances of water, which have an oversized impact in an otherwise water-thrifty garden.

In the Moorish garden tradition (no matter your garden's style), consider adding a focal-point water feature, preferably visible from a central point in the garden and also from a prominent window in the house, so that you can get double the enjoyment from it. A simple vessel of water is all that's needed. Filled to the rim, a steel, copper, or ceramic bowl mirrors the sky, irresistibly drawing the eye and visually cooling the hottest day. Such "brimming bowls," as landscape architect Christine Ten Eyck dubs them, suggest that water is abundant even when it isn't, and they use the least amount of water for greatest effect. In the smallest spaces, a birdbath can suffice quite nicely, whether raised on a pedestal or set like a shiny jewel in a grassy groundcover.

A container pond is another way to bring a symbolic water feature into an otherwise water-conserving garden. Galvanized steel stock tanks—livestock watering tanks, which are commonly sold at farm-supply stores—are easy to turn into container ponds, requiring only a firm, level foundation and occasional topping off with collected rainwater to create a glassy still pond

Left: A Moorish tiled fountain and rill create an oasis in a dry-climate garden.

Right: A brimming bowl can be as simple as a birdbath filled with water.

Clockwise from top left:
By sealing the drainage
hole at the bottom,
you can turn a glazed
ceramic pot into a
miniature pond.

An overscaled
brimming bowl in an
otherwise water-thrifty
garden has symbolic
power.

Stock tanks are easy
to turn into container
ponds.

A water feature need
not be large to have
impact.

or, with the addition of a pump, a bubbling fountain. If you do include a fountain, keep water loss to a minimum by placing it in the center of your container pond, where moving water is unlikely to blow or splash out, or by using a bubbler pump that moves water only a few inches above the pond's surface with almost no splashing at all.

Recirculating fountains, also known as disappearing fountains, are even easier to set up and maintain. Generally they consist of a large, glazed ceramic pot filled with water that spills over the rim and into a hidden reservoir buried in the ground. A pump recirculates the water via a pipe threaded through the center of the pot and sealed against leaks. Such water features can be very beautiful—perfect for symbolizing and showing reverence for a scarce resource.

water feature safety and maintenance

* Purchase mosquito dunks, which organically prevent mosquito larvae in water from maturing into adults, and drop one in your bowl water feature or container pond once a month during mosquito season to keep the pests at bay. For shallow birdbaths, simply spray them out and refill daily.

* If young children visit your home or garden, don't install an open water feature, which can be a drowning hazard. Opt instead for a recirculating fountain in which the water basin is hidden beneath a sturdy grate and river rocks.

* Container ponds can, like natural ponds, achieve a natural balance that requires no chemicals if you include a mix of underwater filtering plants and surface-shading plants like water lilies, with a handful of easy-care fish like *Gambusia* to snack on mosquito larvae. Without plants, you'll need a pump and filter and possibly chemical treatments to keep the water clear.

water-evoking plants

In the 1800s, American pioneers driving wagon trains west across the Great Plains glimpsed in the rolling, tall-grass prairie an echo of the ocean.

"As I looked about me I felt that the grass was the country, as the water is the sea," wrote Nebraskan Willa Cather in *My Ántonia*. "The red of the grass made all the great prairie the colour of winestains, or of certain seaweeds when they are first washed up. And there was so much motion in it; the whole country seemed, somehow, to be running." Through undulating, grassy waves, voyagers sailed across this strange new sea on their canvas-topped wagons, affectionately dubbed prairie schooners.

As the pioneers recognized, grasses evoke the movement of water so well that a horizon-wide view of them can make us feel as if we are at sea. Grasses aren't the only plants, however, that suggest water. Many others share this quality, whether through cascading or fountain-like form, or through color that, when massed, brings to mind a river or pool, or even through an uncanny resemblance to undersea life like coral and seaweed. Savvy, creative gardeners can use such plants in their water-saving gardens to create an illusion of watery abundance. Choosing dry-adapted plants to accomplish this sleight of hand makes the illusion even more satisfying.

A grassy hillside garden is threaded with ribbons of flowering perennials.

Let's dive into this gardening magician's trick, starting with plants whose form echoes water in some fashion. Do you want to make waves in your garden? Grasses, as our pioneer ancestors knew, are perfect candidates, and many are native or well adapted to dry and hot-summer climates. Grasses and grasslike plants of all sizes can be massed to introduce a sense of watery movement in the garden, especially on breezy days. For low-growing waves, nothing beats sedges (*Carex* spp.), whose floppy, mop-top habit grows into a tufty meadow. While some sedges love moist soil, many varieties thrive in dry shade or sun, like Berkeley sedge (*Carex divulsa*), Texas sedge (*C. texensis*), and Pennsylvania sedge (*C. pensylvanica*). Likewise, monkey grasses (*Liriope* spp. and *Ophiopogon* spp.), which thrive in warm southern and coastal climates, make waves of strappy, deep-green or pale-striped foliage. Low-water eco-lawns—fine fescues are suited to cool-summer climates, plains-native buffalograss (*Bouteloua dactyloides*) to hot-summer climates—if mown only a few times a year, seem to flow along the ground like gentle ocean swells. You need not sod your entire yard with such grasses; make a circular "pond" or amoeba-shaped "pool" of it for a

Rippling like water in a stony creek, Mexican feathergrass (*Nassella tenuissima*) undulates in the lightest breeze.

smaller but still evocative look. For a more dramatic look, if you wish to conjure the illusion of billowing, storm-tossed waves, use taller ornamental grasses: cloud-like bamboo muhly (*Muhlenbergia dumosa*), hair-textured Mexican feathergrass (*Nassella tenuissima*), nodding northern or inland sea oats (*Chasmanthium latifolium*), blue-green big muhly (*Muhlenbergia lindheimeri*), rosy love grass (*Eragrostis spectabilis*), and cotton-candy-colored Gulf muhly (*Muhlenbergia capillaris*), among many others.

If you have a deft hand with hedge pruners and enjoy a bit of whimsy, you might add rolling waves to your garden through topiary. Dutch plantsman Piet Oudolf's famous wavy hedge popularized this look, which has since taken hold in many incarnations throughout the world. Any dense-leaved shrub that responds well to hedging, like boxwood, will work. Just choose one that doesn't require heavy watering once established. Over time, sculpt

A wavy clipped hedge brings to mind ocean swells.

the top of the hedge into a series of crested, pointy waves or soft, undulating billows, whichever strikes your fancy, and your garden will never feel water-deprived.

Would you like to have a spraying fountain without the maintenance of an electric water pump? Plants can play that role too. Choose upright grasses and other plants with an arching or vase-shaped form. Planted singly, rather than en masse, fountain-shaped plants gain power through contrast with other forms, like mounds, cones, or sprawling groundcovers, so don't be afraid to mix it up around your living fountain. The effect is enhanced through color contrast as well. If your fountain plant has dark foliage, choose something bright behind it, or vice versa, to highlight the spraying form. Grasses that work especially well include the appropriately named fountain grass (*Pennisetum* spp.), 'Blonde Ambition' blue grama (*Bouteloua gracilis*), purple moor grass (*Molinia* spp.), prairie dropseed (*Sporobolus heterolepis*), maiden grass (*Miscanthus* spp.), and Mexican feathergrass (*Nassella tenuissima*). In addition to grasses, dry-adapted plants with a fountain-like habit include yuccas, which are generally cold hardy, and cordylines and phormiums, which are not. Try coppery pink 'Evening Glow' phormium, with an arching, spreading "spray"; nontrunking 'Electric Pink' cordyline, with hot-pink and maroon stripes; and strappy, blue-green softleaf yucca (*Yucca recurvifolia*).

Pennisetum in bloom resembles a fountain's spray, while taller miscanthus grasses evoke a cresting wave.

Cascading plants can create the illusion of a spilling waterfall, especially when planted in tall pots and hanging planters or atop walls or rock formations, where their flowing habit can be shown off to greatest advantage. Choose among dry-tolerant creeping and matting groundcovers like woolly stemodia (*Stemodia lanata*), silver ponyfoot (*Dichondra argentea* 'Silver Falls'), and trailing lantana (*Lantana montevidensis*); sprawling woody perennials like prostrate rosemary (*Rosmarinus officinalis* 'Prostratus'); and grassy clumpers like spaghetti-leaved Texas beargrass (*Nolina texana*). And don't overlook the many succulents that seem designed to imitate falling water: the steady, moss-green drip of string-of-pearls (*Senecio rowleyanus*); the splashing effect of upturned leaves on string-of-fishhooks (*Senecio radicans*); the fleshy-leaved and pink-flowered cascade of baby sunrose (*Aptenia cordifolia*); and the rivulets of bottlebrush-textured burro's tail sedum (*Sedum morganianum*).

Texas beargrass (*Nolina texana*) spills like a waterfall from a planting pocket in a boulder-strewn bed.

Weeping trees have the power to evoke the presence of water in the garden too, even if they're actually quite happy growing in dry conditions. With pendant limbs and leaves that droop with a waterfall's grace, they bring to mind the water-loving weeping willow, which is often found alongside streams and ponds. What a trick, then, to use that drooping form to fool the mind into imagining a nearby creek or pool! You'll find weeping trees for every climate, deciduous and evergreen, with a rich range of foliage color, from green to burgundy to icy blue. Weeping acacia (*Acacia pendula*), a graceful tree with long, silver-green leaves that flutter in the breeze, prefers hot summers, mild winters, and well-drained soil, making it a dry-garden doppelgänger of the weeping willow. Shoestring acacia (*Acacia stenophylla*) has a similar look with even skinnier leaves, plus seedpods that look like a string of green peas. Also for mild-winter climates, the pendulous branches

the water-saving garden

of weeping bottlebrush (*Callistemon viminalis*) blush at their tips with crimson, bristle-shaped flowers in spring and summer. In regions with cooler winters, weeping yaupon holly (*Ilex vomitoria* 'Pendula') presents a versatile, narrow profile, with stiffly draped, evergreen branches bedecked with scarlet berries in winter. Weeping mulberry is a diminutive tree with curtain-like branches that sweep the ground and enclose a fun hideout in a children's garden. *Morus alba* 'Chaparral' is the nonfruiting male cultivar; *Morus alba* 'Pendula' is the female, with messy but edible fruit. Perhaps the most unusual choice is weeping blue atlas cedar (*Cedrus atlantica* 'Glauca Pendula'). Spookily hunched, draping silvery-blue needles to the ground, this evergreen eventually grows to the size of a city bus, by which point it seems to be stretching arms draped in tattered robes to snag passersby. With that kind of drama, who needs an actual waterfall?

Vines on vertical trellises make good virtual waterfalls too, even though they're actually climbing skyward. In hot-summer climates, vines can be especially useful as living awnings, trained onto trellises attached to multistory buildings, where they function like cooling waterfalls of foliage, or on patio arbors for shaded garden seating. Across horizontal spans, long tendrils often cascade downward, and if flowers or fruits—grapes and gourds, for example—droop invitingly from above, they simply add to the water-spill effect. Try evergreen, orange-flowering 'Tangerine Beauty' crossvine (*Bignonia capreolata*); fall-blooming butterfly vine (*Mascagnia macroptera*), with chrome-yellow flowers and papery, butterfly-shaped seedpods; vigorous Lady Banks rose (*Rosa banksiae*), whose sprawling canes are smothered in frilly yellow or white flowers in springtime; and Mexican snapdragon vine (*Maurandella antirrhiniflora*), a dainty but drought-tolerant vine with lavender flowers in summer.

Clockwise from top left: String of nickels (*Dischidia nummularia*) seems to stream out of a pot into a gravel "pond" outlined with river rock.

Like jellyfish ascending into the trees, hanging plastic domes support "tentacled" burro's tail sedum (*Sedum morganianum*).

Drought-tolerant acacia in a "pool" of silver ponyfoot resembles a weeping willow at the water's edge.

This page: A metal scrim overlays this campus building in Mesa, Arizona, supporting grape ivy (*Cissus trifoliata*) that provides cooling shade.

Left: Woolly stemodia
(*Stemodia lanata*)
resembles a frothy,
silver-blue pool.

Right: Silver ponyfoot
(*Dichondra argentea*)
shimmers like a moonlit
pond.

Waves, fountains, and waterfalls build excitement into a garden, even if they're made of plants. But you can also plant a tranquil, cooling pond. Mat-forming or creeping groundcovers with silver or blue foliage quickly fill in to create the illusion of a limpid pool or a light-reflecting lake, while covering bare soil or replacing swaths of lawn. Dry-adapted silver groundcovers include woolly stemodia (*Stemodia lanata*), a fast spreader with silvery green leaves and tiny purple flowers in summer; silver ponyfoot (*Dichondra argentea*), with cloven, dusted-pewter leaves; lamb's ear (*Stachys byzantina*), with pettable, fuzzy foliage; and silver carpet (*Dymondia margaretae*), with narrow, silver-and-white leaves that lie nearly flat along the ground. For lakes of green, try trailing verbena (*Verbena canadensis* 'Homestead Purple'), with emerald, coarse-textured leaves topped by royal-purple flowers; John Creech stonecrop (*Sedum spurium* 'John Creech'), with green, scalloped leaves adorned with a haze of pink flowers in late summer; and Turkish speedwell (*Veronica liwanensis*), with glossy, disc-shaped leaves topped with tiny blue flowers in spring. As wildflower enthusiasts know, you can also make a floriferous, if short-lived, blue lagoon by sowing seeds of annuals like Texas bluebonnet (*Lupinus texensis*) and other lupines,

California bluebell (*Phacelia campanularia*), and blue flax (*Linum lewisii*). For a frosty blue pond that never ices over, try a low-growing, evergreen shrub with a puddling form, like *Juniperus squamata* 'Blue Star'.

Would you prefer a meandering stream? Choose a long-blooming perennial with blue or purple flowers that grows to between 1 and 3 feet tall. Mass it by the dozens in a ribbon running through the garden, after first ensuring that surrounding plants will grow no taller than your chosen plant and that sun and shade conditions are consistent for the entire "stream." This effect works best when you have some height for overlooking the garden, perhaps from a deck or elevated patio. Good candidates, depending on your climate, include plumbago (*Plumbago auriculata*), blue false indigo (*Baptisia australis*), salvia (*Salvia* x *sylvestris* 'May Night' or *Salvia* x *sylvestris* 'Blue Hill'), catmint (*Nepeta* x *faassenii* 'Walker's Low'), and lavender (*Lavandula angustifolia* or *Lavandula stoechas*).

The Salvia River at Chicago's Lurie Garden is made up of four types of purple and blue salvia.

Left: A mermaid poses in an under-the-sea succulent garden. The blue-painted fence enhances the illusion.

Right: Blue glass beads sub for water and succulents for water lilies in this dish planter.

Plants with an otherworldly form or fantastical foliage or color can create a magical underwater mood, much to a visitor's delighted surprise. Succulents are especially good for this, which is ironic because they are wonderfully water-thrifty plants. Massed in an undulating rock garden, a colorful assortment of succulents can imitate an under-the-sea garden so convincingly that a clownfish might feel at home. This is a trick that only those in frost-free climates can pull off in in-ground gardens, but elsewhere you can use container plants, which can be brought indoors in winter, to similar effect. Mix a variety of succulents for the best effect, massing multiples of the low growers and generously accenting the scene with taller specimens. Look for clamshell-shaped paddle plant (*Kalanchoe luciae*); frilly echeverias in a slew of pastel colors, which look, en masse, like a bed of coral; agaves with writhing arms, like the appropriately named squid agave (*Agave bracteosa*) and octopus agave (*A. vilmoriniana*); blue chalksticks (*Senecio serpens*) for soft-fingered anemones; *Euphorbia horrida*, which, when small, resembles spiny-balled sea urchins; rosy, branching 'Sticks on Fire' euphorbia to mimic red sea whip; crested euphorbia for undulating brain coral; and small aloes for sea grass. Once you start looking, you'll see sea creatures and coral reef plants everywhere you look on the succulent tables at the nursery. Branch out into the perennial section and add a few foxtail ferns (*Asparagus densiflorus* 'Myers')—so reminiscent of Sideshow Bob's hairdo on *The Simpsons*—which can double as feathery arms of seaweed in an underwater-theme garden.

You can also use succulents to create an ever-blooming, waterless lily pond in a container or birdbath. Start with a glazed ceramic pot (blue is good for evoking the color of water) or a birdbath and fill it with a sharp-draining potting mix for succulents or, even better, make your own out of potting soil, perlite or chicken grit, and coarse sand. Be sure the pot has holes for drainage; if you use a birdbath, drill a few drainage holes and mound up the soil above the rim so that plants sit high enough to prevent root rot. Choose an odd number of dinner plate aeoniums (*Aeonium tabuliforme*), with flat saucers resembling lily pads, and a handful of dusty pink and blue-green echeverias for the water lily flowers. If aeoniums don't appreciate your climate's summer heat, use echeverias mixed with smaller sempervivums with white centers for added sparkle. Mulch the "pond" with blue or green frosted-glass chips or glass beads for a watery finishing touch.

An under-sea garden is composed of succulents chosen for their resemblance to coral-reef creatures. A kinetic fish sculpture completes the illusion.

squeezing water from stone

When a river runs dry, a bed of tumbled-smooth rocks is exposed. Behind every waterfall stands a skeletal structure of ledges and slabs of stone.

And although it's a common idiom that nothing is less likely than squeezing water from a stone, the fact is that stone and water share an intimate connection in nature, a connection we can exploit in our gardens by using carefully arranged stone to suggest the presence of water. It's one more visual trick we can use to evoke water without actually using any.

gravel seas and pools

Japanese Zen gardens, which originated more than five hundred years ago as temple gardens for spiritual contemplation, featured stone-as-water illusions that work well in modern or Japanese-style gardens today. Interestingly, while water is essential to a Japanese garden, Zen gardens prove that this visual element need not consist of actual H_2O. Instead, an expanse of white or gray gravel, painstakingly raked into rippling lines, represents water, which "breaks" around boulders that stand as islands in the sea. Dry Zen gardens defy Western notions of what a garden should be. They may eschew plants altogether, relying instead on a diorama-like composition of boulders and gravel. Despite their evident aridity,

A reflective "pond" is actually a mirror set in sand, an illusion revealed by the homeowner's pet cat.

In a Zen garden, boulders rise like islands in a sea of raked gravel.

such gardens hold a deep symbolism for water in their carefully selected and arranged elements. This symbolism goes deeper than a simple representation of the natural world, however. Gravel represents a body of water—a river or the sea—but the illusory movement of the water may represent the human journey from birth to death. The whole becomes an object to meditate upon.

Whether or not you appreciate the Zen garden's symbolism, the use of gravel to evoke water in a dry garden works well today, especially with the geometry of contemporary homes and the horizontal lines of ranch- or rambler-style houses. Modern interpretations have unhappily sometimes devolved into gravel spread across the entire yard, a bleak vision that probably instigated the tongue-in-cheek use of "zero-scape" for "xeriscape." An undifferentiated expanse of gravel will never conjure the rippling movement or visual cooling power of water. It'll just look like a moonscape—and will sizzle like an oven in summer. The secret to the illusion is to use gravel in a relatively small area as a flowing negative space (much in the way lawn may be used), accented with attractive boulders of varying heights, and framed by softening plants—or, if you prefer traditional Zen garden style, enclosed by a wall or bamboo-screen fence. The boulders are a key part of the illusion, as they make "islands" from

the water-saving garden

which the "water" ripples outward. Choose at least three large, naturally shaped stones—big enough that you'll likely need a skid-steer loader to place them—all of the same type of rock, selecting for character and beauty. One vertical and two horizontal boulders arranged in a scalene triangle (with unequal sides and angles) is pleasing. Set at least one-third of each stone into the ground to create a natural look, and encircle them with raked ripples of crushed gravel. Or you may prefer to forgo the contemplative but frequent raking and just enjoy the flat plane of gravel as it seems to wash around the boulders.

Left: A boulder "pond" supports 3 metal cattails—evoking water with only stone and steel.

Right: A modern, Western interpretation of a Zen garden combines clipped boxwood and gravel raked into ripples around a lantern "island."

stone waterfalls

A dry waterfall is another creative way to introduce the idea of water, especially if it "flows" into a gravel pool at its base. Like the raked-gravel sea, this idea is also borrowed from the Japanese garden tradition. Dry waterfalls may be built into a natural slope with boulders and flat ledges

of stone set partially into the soil to hold them in place, or, more abstractly, symbolized in a flat garden by a careful arrangement of vertical standing stones tucked into the corner of a Zen gravel garden. Working with stone is an art, especially to create an illusion of water, so do your homework and study images of wet and dry waterfalls before starting. Stone provides the framework of a waterfall, and, even when dry, should visually flow like water, with natural irregularities as it drops to the lowest level. Don't hesitate to hire experienced help when placing heavy stones either vertically or on a slope. If not set properly—that is, deeply enough in the soil to avoid movement over time—stone can shift and fall, causing serious injury. Boulders should be set securely enough to withstand pushing or climbing as well as the pressure of waterlogged soil after a rain.

pebble mosaic paths

With a bit of artistry and lots of patience, you can lay a mosaic path of smooth pebbles to suggest a flowing river. Pebble mosaic paving is commonly found in Asian courtyard gardens, but it makes a beautiful path in any type of garden. The simplest designs use only one color and size of stone and are laid in subtle swirls and wavy lines; the most complex use pebbles in multiple colors and sizes laid in intricate arrangements. Bagged river rock (1-inch stones are easy to work with) is available at most landscape supply yards, or you can take buckets to a stone yard and sort through the bulk piles to select your own stones in various colors. If you do this, take a container of water with you in order to wash the pebbles and reveal their true colors. If you hope to use stones collected from hikes or beach trips, please think twice. It's illegal to remove rocks from national or state parks, and while most of us have brought home a souvenir pebble or two, a mosaic path requires thousands.

Wash your pebbles to clean off dust and dirt, spread them out on a clean sheet or cardboard, and let them dry. Lay out your path with marking paint and, assuming you live in a mild-winter climate, excavate to about 5 inches deep. In cold-winter climates that experience frost heaving, you may need a deeper base for your path; check local recommendations. Spread 2 inches of paver base, which you can buy by the bag at home-improvement stores, and compact it with a tamper. Next, install edging that will hold the sides of the path in place; flexible bender board or steel landscape edging will work. Make sure your edging is level with the desired height of your path to avoid a tripping hazard. For setting the stones in mortar, it's important to avoid working on a hot, sunny day because the mortar will dry too quickly. Choose a cool, cloudy day, and complete one small section at a time. Mix a batch of mortar (not concrete) and spread it in a 3-inch layer atop the compacted paver base. Press the pebbles on edge, lengthwise, into the mortar, which gives strength to the design before most of the stone is set. You don't want pebbles to pop out later after all your hard work. Before the mortar dries, lay a thick piece of plywood on it and press evenly with your feet to ensure that the stones are all level. Next, use a gentle spray of water from the hose to clean mortar off the exposed surface of the pebbles,

the water-saving garden

revealing its natural coloring. Keep each completed section damp by spraying it a couple times a day for several days, allowing it to cure slowly, which makes for a stronger hold.

Obviously, a mosaic path is a time-intensive and laborious project. But you can also make smaller-scale, water-evoking mosaics around focal-point pots or water features, and if they won't be walked upon, you can skip the mortar. Just know that dry-laid stones will likely sink or be displaced over time, and prepare to do a little touch-up work on your creation now and then.

dry streams

The falling or rippling movement of a gravel waterfall or sea is, of course, illusory, but a dry stream provides both the illusion and reality of a watercourse. Designed to look like a streambed that's run dry, it chatters to life when it rains, channeling runoff safely away from the home's foundation and through the garden. Throughout the West, dry streams occur naturally and make interesting areas to explore, for both rock hounds and native-plant enthusiasts. In a dry stream, arroyo, or wash, as they're variously known, seasonal flooding provides extra moisture, enabling a greater diversity of plants, including trees, to thrive that might not get enough water elsewhere. On a smaller scale, a dry stream works beautifully in a garden setting, not only to fool the eye into imagining a flowing stream but also to address erosion and runoff that occur when water washes through from a neighbor's lot, a nearby hillside, or a paved parking lot up the road. For this reason, dry streams are popular garden features in both arid and rainy parts of the country.

Digging out a dry stream is simple. Making it look natural is an art. Part of the art is constructing the streambed to look as if it's occurred naturally rather than randomly plunked down. Before putting shovel to soil, study how water moves across your property during a heavy rain. If you have erosion problems, as evidenced by gouges in the soil and exposed roots of plants, you'll be able to see the path that runoff takes. But if your dry stream is to be more decorative—more for illusion than runoff management—do still take the time to study water patterns when it rains. Your stream should

Left: Blue glass evokes water pooling amid river rocks.

Right: Blue-gray river rock laid in a swirling pattern creates the illusion of a flowing stream.

the water-saving garden

flow through low spots in your garden, meandering gently around obstacles like trees, berms, and large rocks as it goes. Remember, water always seeks the lowest level. Depending on your specific conditions, you may wish to construct a dry stream that captures runoff from a downspout or excess flow from a rain barrel, slowing it down with large river rocks and small boulders, before funneling the water into a rain garden that can hold and slowly absorb excess water. It may be tempting to send the water straight out to the street and from there into stormwater drains, but as discussed in chapter 1, that can create another set of problems. If your lot is steep and small, requiring that water be moved off-property to avoid damage to your home, at least try to retain some of it along the way. For high-volume situations, be sure to consult with a drainage engineer or a landscaper experienced in handling runoff to ensure you don't create a problem for your downhill neighbor.

As for aesthetic design, a dry stream at least 3 to 5 feet wide looks better than a skinny, ribbon-like stream. Width and depth determine how much water your stream can hold, but a relatively shallow, wide stream is better able to slow water than a narrow, deeper channel. Broadly meandering curves also work to slow the flow of water, plus they lend a natural appearance. Since water doesn't like to make tight turns, especially when flowing quickly, be sure to smooth out curves into broad arcs. Depth and width will need to be decided based on your particular conditions, but, in general, a channel depth of 12 to 15 inches works well. Once you've excavated, line the bottom of your stream with water-permeable landscape fabric to keep rocks from sinking into the soil over time. Choose river rock and boulders that are quarried locally or within a few hundred miles, because these will blend with the larger landscape and help your dry stream look natural. River rock should be chunky enough that it won't be picked up by the flow of water during a heavy rain; palm-sized or slightly smaller stones are generally a good choice. Place larger boulders of varying sizes along the edges of your watercourse; you can set two or three smaller boulders close together for the effect of one larger stone. Take the time to set the boulders partially in the soil along the stream's edge, burying each stone to a depth of at least one-third, as they would occur naturally, rather than plopping them on top of the river rock. Also avoid laying them in a line, string-of-pearls fashion;

A dry stream winds through a gravel garden abloom with wildflowers and a Lady Banks rose.

a random scattering looks more natural. Your goal is to create the illusion of boulders that have been tumbled to the edges over time. Place the largest boulders along the outer curves of your stream; these function as natural obstacles that the water is forced to go around. You can also place a large boulder in "midstream," like an island that splits the flow of water for a few moments. For added utility, you may wish to lay naturally shaped but flat stones in a meandering course through the center of the stream, to serve as a path when conditions are dry. Set these flush with the river rock so that they don't impede the flow of water when it rains.

It can be difficult to keep lawn grass from insinuating itself into crevices and openings along a rock-lined dry stream. To avoid this maintenance headache, create generously sized garden beds along both sides, and choose plants that aren't aggressive creepers. As an added bonus, you'll be eliminating portions of thirsty lawn in the process, and your dry stream will appear more realistic surrounded by plants that seem to thrive on the extra water available streamside. Enhance the illusion even further, if you wish, by including a bridge that crosses the dry stream—a necessary feature if the stream cuts across a path in your garden. This can be as simple as a few stepping stones spaced across the "creek" or a thick stone slab laid across a narrow span, or as complex as a wooden or steel footbridge.

glass rivers and ponds

A sort of manmade stone, glass can be used to evoke water in the garden too. Tumbled to smooth any sharp edges, colored chips of glass in blue or green make eye-catching, stylized streams or pools that work especially well in clean-lined contemporary and desert gardens. Colored glass can also substitute for water in a birdbath, for example. There's a playfulness in it, or perhaps a sense of irony. *I know no one is going to be fooled*, it seems to say, *but I'll make you think of water anyway.*

Glass with baked-in color, rather than a painted finish, is fade resistant, even in bright sun. Blues and greens tend to be especially long lasting, and they're best for conjuring the illusion of water. I suppose you could smash your own collection of empty wine bottles and use the shards, but I wouldn't advise it. Jagged pieces of glass aren't barefoot friendly or safe. Instead, look for landscaping glass, sometimes called glass rock, which can be purchased by the bag online and is sometimes offered at city recycling centers. Made of recycled bottles and household glass, it's melted down, custom colored, crushed, and tumbled. For very small applications you can also use vase fillers sold at home-décor stores: frosted and tumbled glass chips and sparkling glass beads are readily available. Tumbled glass can be safely walked on barefoot, just like gravel (first install water-permeable landscape fabric to keep the glass from sinking into the soil over time), but the best water-evoking effect comes not from making paths or patios with it, which can be visually overwhelming, but from using it strategically to mimic a small pond or stream. (This is more affordable too, as landscaping glass isn't cheap.) Even a small amount spread in an irregular circle around a tall pot or island-like rock can make a big impact. Keep in mind that leaves and

Left: Crushed blue glass in two colors mulches a raised round planter, where agaves seem to float like water lilies.

Right: Green glass chips substitute for water in a purely decorative birdbath.

other tree litter that falls into your glass "water feature" will require regular raking or blowing, just as if you'd used gravel, so select a treeless, sunny area if possible.

Unlike colored glass, which flaunts its artificiality, a mirror actually fools the eye into seeing something that isn't there. Water is a natural mirror; think of how a still pool reflects the sky. Just so, a circular or rectangular mirror placed flat on the ground can make an eye-fooling faux pond (see page 182). Prepare the ground by digging down a few inches and laying a cushioning bed of sand as a foundation for your mirror. Carefully arrange fist-sized or larger river rocks of varying sizes along the edges of the mirror, naturalistically softening sharp corners if you used rectangular glass. Next, plant around your faux pond, using low-growing sedges, ornamental grasses, and any other low-water plants that convey the idea of a pondside garden. Be sure your surrounding planting bed sits slightly higher than the level of your mirror, to enhance the illusion; after all, water always finds the lowest spot. (Since a mirror will break, perhaps painfully, if stepped on, do consider whether a mirror pond is suitable for your garden, especially if you have children or large pets.) Your new "pool" will be sure to fool visitors until they peer into it to look for fish and catch their own reflection smiling back at them.

A paver with a fish design, surrounded by glass beads, adds a note of watery whimsy to a stone patio.

part five

101 PLANTS for
water-saving gardens

Choosing plants for your water-saving garden can be daunting, especially if you're new to gardening or have recently moved to an unfamiliar climate in a region with local flora you don't know. Consider the following list as a jumping-off point for your own research into appropriate, hardy, and beautiful plants for your garden. Organized by type—trees; shrubs; perennials; grasses and sedges; woody lilies, succulents, and cacti; palms and cycads; groundcovers; vines; bulbs; and annuals—these plants were selected for all regions of the United States and USDA hardiness zones, although those suited to drier regions, where water conservation is particularly critical, are more heavily represented.

Hardiness zones (which indicate cold tolerance) and light preferences, though helpful to know, tell only part of the story about whether a plant is suitable for any particular region. Heat tolerance matters too, especially for southern or southwestern gardeners. And a tolerance for dry soil means one thing in Minnesota and quite another in New Mexico. Therefore, use the growing information provided for each plant as a first step in determining whether it's likely to grow well in your garden. Start with hardiness zone, and if that matches up for you, do an online search of the plant by botanical name and your city or state to learn whether it grows well in your region, or check with your local extension service or a trusted local nursery. When you have a match—the plant grows well in drought-tolerant gardens in your region—then consider the light conditions it needs and site it accordingly. A sun-loving plant will never thrive in shade and vice versa. You'll have much better success if you choose plants for the light conditions you have. And if you goof, as even experienced gardeners do, and you see that a plant isn't thriving where you've placed it, don't be afraid to move it to a better spot to see if it'll perk up.

Although every plant on this list grows well without heavy watering, and many need little or no supplemental watering in years with normal rainfall, remember that all plants need regular water during the first year to become well established (with the exception of cacti and other dryland plants, which generally just need a deep watering at planting and then occasional soakings during the first summer). Sharp drainage is also crucial for most dry-adapted plants, although those that can handle seasonal flooding are noted here as good choices for rain gardens.

Any plant list for a country as large and climatically diverse as the United States will invariably include some considered invasive in certain regions. And just because a plant is considered invasive (that is, likely to escape cultivation into the wild and outcompete native plants) doesn't mean you won't find it in the garden center. Do the right thing for your area's native habitats and wild spaces: check local invasive-plant lists and avoid buying or planting invasive plants.

Purple coneflower and bee balm attract pollinators—and the family pet.

TREES

'BLUE ICE' ARIZONA CYPRESS

Cupressus arizonica 'Blue Ice'
Size: 20 to 30 feet tall by 10 to
15 feet wide
Zones: 7–10
Prefers: Full sun; average to dry,
well-drained soil

With frosty blue needles and a
Christmas-tree fragrance, this fast-
growing Arizona native thrives in
hot, sunny conditions. The relatively
narrow profile of the 'Blue Ice' cultivar
fits well in most residential yards so
long as you avoid planting it under
power lines. Makes an excellent
windbreak or specimen tree.

BUR OAK

Quercus macrocarpa
Size: 60 to 100 feet tall and wide
Zones: 3–8
Prefers: Full to part sun; moist to
dry soil

Had he lived in the New World,
Newton might have discovered gravity
by sitting under a bur oak, which in
autumn drops fringed acorns the size
of golf balls. Fast-growing for an oak,
this mighty tree eventually shades both
house and garden; choose with care
if your lot is small. Resistance to oak
wilt makes it a good choice where the
disease is prevalent.

CRAPE MYRTLE

Lagerstroemia indica
Size: 10 to 40 feet tall by 15 to 25 feet
wide, depending on cultivar
Zones: 7–9
Prefers: Full sun; average, well-
drained soil

Embraced throughout the South for
its nonstop summer blooms—pink,
red, lilac, and white are common—and
vase-shaped form, crape myrtle also
delivers with golden or red leaves
in fall and muscular, mottled trunks
with peeling bark in winter. Choose
carefully by size to avoid a compulsion
to drastically prune—that is, to commit
"crape murder"—later on. Never top
its branches, which destroys the tree's
graceful shape.

DESERT WILLOW

Chilopsis linearis
Size: 15 to 20 feet tall and wide
Zones: 7–10
Prefers: Full sun; dry, infertile,
well-drained soil

Showy, trumpet-shaped flowers
ranging from pale pink to burgundy
adorn this airy tree all summer,
attracting hummingbirds galore.
Narrow, willow-like leaves cast light
shade, and pencil-thin seedpods dangle
from the branches after flowers fade
and leaves drop. It likes water about
as much as a cat does, so give it good
drainage and avoid regular irrigation
once established.

Cupressus arizonica
'Blue Ice'

ESCARPMENT LIVE OAK

Quercus fusiformis

Size: 20 to 40 feet tall by 25 to 40 feet wide

Zones: 7–10

Prefers: Full sun to part sun; average to dry, well-drained soil

With contorted limbs, a spreading, dense canopy, and more width than height, stately escarpment live oak adds gravitas to the garden. Popularly considered evergreen, it drops its oval, shiny, gray-green leaves all at once in spring just before new leaves emerge. In California, the native *Quercus agrifolia* is a better choice.

MEXICAN BUCKEYE

Ungnadia speciosa

Size: 12 to 30 feet tall by 8 to 12 feet wide

Zones: 7–9

Prefers: Sun, part shade, or dappled shade; average to dry, well-drained soil

This graceful small tree erupts with pink blossoms in spring, which appear alongside narrow chartreuse leaves. In autumn, dangling, rounded seedpods resembling buckeyes emerge to enliven bare branches all winter.

PALO VERDE

Parkinsonia microphylla (yellow palo verde) and *P. florida* (blue palo verde)

Size: 15 to 30 feet tall by 15 to 20 feet wide

Zones: 8–11

Prefers: Full sun; average to dry, infertile, well-drained soil

This airy desert tree blazes yellow in spring like bottled sunshine in a dark room. Its unusual green trunk and branches can photosynthesize if drought causes leaf drop. Overwatering results in weak growth, so irrigate rarely once established. *Parkinsonia* x 'Desert Museum', a thornless hybrid, grows as far east as central Texas.

PERSIMMON

Diospyros virginiana

Size: 35 to 60 feet tall by 25 to 35 feet wide

Zones: 4–9

Prefers: Full sun to part shade; average to dry soil; suitable for rain gardens

Distinctive, deeply fissured gray bark makes this tree as attractive in winter as it is in summer and fall, when female trees produce orange, sweet-tasting fruits. In drier climates to the west, try smaller Texas persimmon (*Diospyros texana*), which has silvery gray bark and round black fruits.

POMEGRANATE

Punica granatum
Size: 6 to 20 feet tall by 4 to
15 feet wide
Zones: 8–11
Prefers: Full sun to part shade; average
to dry soil

Usually grown for its tasty red fruits,
pomegranate also makes an attractive,
multitrunked specimen tree or bushy
shrub appropriate for hedging. Frilly
orange flowers in spring ripen into
large leathery fruits, which hang like
Christmas balls amid butter-yellow
fall foliage.

REDBUD

Cercis canadensis var. *canadensis*
(eastern redbud), *C. canadensis*
var. *texensis* (Texas redbud), and
C. canadensis var. *mexicana*
(Mexican redbud)
Size: 10 to 30 feet tall by 20 to 35 feet
wide, depending on species
Zones: 4–8
Prefers: Full sun, part shade, or dappled
shade; average to dry soil

A pink haze settles over the bare
branches of this small, deciduous tree
in early spring, blushing in a rosy-
purple profusion before giving way to
glossy, heart-shaped green leaves. Fall
color is minimal.

STRAWBERRY TREE

Arbutus 'Marina'
Size: 20 to 40 feet tall by 20 to
30 feet wide
Zones: 7–9
Prefers: Full sun to part shade; dry,
well-drained soil

A slow-growing, evergreen cousin
of the native California madrone,
strawberry tree gets its name from
dangling orange and red fruit that
vaguely resembles strawberries.
Drooping pink flowers, leathery dark-
green leaves, flaking cinnamon-red
bark, and sinuous trunks make it a
stunning ornamental for every season.

TEXAS MOUNTAIN LAUREL

Sophora secundiflora
Size: 15 to 30 feet tall by 10 feet wide
Zones: 8–9
Prefers: Full sun to part shade; average
to dry, well-drained soil

In spring this handsome, glossy-leaved
evergreen appears to be draped in
a wisteria vine. Heavy clusters of
purple blossoms droop from every
branch, with a fragrance exactly like
grape Kool-Aid. Black, segmented
seedpods that hang on through winter
hold bright-red seeds that, while
prettily resembling necklace beads,
are poisonous.

Cercis canadensis var.
texensis

YELLOWWOOD

Cladrastis kentukea

Size: 30 to 50 feet tall by 40 to
55 feet wide
Zones: 4–8
Prefers: Full to part sun; average,
well-drained soil

Orchid-like white flowers cascade
in sweet-smelling clusters in spring,
giving way to long, flat seedpods in fall.
With a neat habit, it makes a good patio
tree or shade tree for a small lot, and
it can be grown in a rain garden, too.
Its only fault is a tendency to split and
break, so prune to eliminate V-shaped
crotch angles.

SHRUBS

AGARITA

Mahonia trifoliolata

Size: 2 to 6 feet tall and wide
Zones: 7–9
Prefers: Full sun to dappled shade;
average to dry, well-drained soil

Branches of prickly, gray-green, holly-
like leaves are accented in spring with
clusters of sweet-smelling yellow
flowers, followed by red berries that
attract birds. A suckering, thicket-like
habit makes it a good natural hedge.

APACHE PLUME

Fallugia paradoxa

Size: 3 to 5 feet tall by 5 to 8 feet wide
Zones: 4–9
Prefers: Full sun; average to dry,
infertile, well-drained soil

It's hard to say which is prettier: the
open, white, rose-like blossoms, which
appear in late spring and summer,
or the feathery pink seed heads with
dark-rose filaments that follow. Place it
where the setting sun will incandesce
the fluffy seed heads. This desert
Southwest shrub appreciates extra
water so long as it has good drainage,
but it dislikes humidity.

CALIFORNIA LILAC

Ceanothus 'Concha'

Size: 5 to 7 feet tall by 6 to 10 feet wide
Zones: 7–10
Prefers: Full sun to part shade; average
to dry, infertile, well-drained soil

The West Coast's answer to blue
French hydrangea, *Ceanothus* makes
gardeners swoon with true-blue flower
clusters atop branches of glossy,
deep-green leaves. Tough love is key.
Coddling with rich soil, fertilizer, or
regular water, especially in summer,
will kill it. *Ceanothus* requires mild
summers and winters to thrive. Many
other cultivars, from groundcovers to
tree form, are also available.

DWARF BOTTLEBRUSH

Callistemon citrinus 'Little John'
Size: 3 to 5 feet tall by 4 to 6 feet wide
Zones: 8–11
Prefers: Full to part sun; average, well-drained soil

Blue-green leaves and a dense, neatly mounded form make this Australian evergreen a knockout in all seasons. But when the flowers appear in spring and summer—cylinders of dark-red stamens tipped with dots of yellow, like a fiber-optic lamp—the effect is electric.

LEWIS' MOCK ORANGE

Philadelphus lewisii
Size: 6 to 12 feet tall and wide
Zones: 5–10
Prefers: Full sun to part shade; moist to dry, well-drained soil

The members of the Lewis and Clark Expedition, who collected this upright, arching shrub on their return journey in 1806, were surely attracted by its snowy white flowers and fruity, sweet fragrance. It's just as appealing in gardens today, either as a loose hedge or along the top edge of a rain garden.

MEXICAN ORCHID TREE

Bauhinia mexicana
Size: 4 to 12 feet tall by 6 to 10 feet wide
Zones: 8b–11
Prefers: Morning sun to part shade; average to dry, well-drained soil

Floppy, white, orchid-shaped flowers bloom sporadically on this small shrubby tree all summer, lighting up the understory and feeding hummingbirds and butterflies. In its northern range, it dies to the ground each winter but returns from the roots. Anacacho orchid tree (*Bauhinia lunarioides*), a spring bloomer with smaller leaves and flowers, is an airy semi-evergreen with slightly better cold tolerance.

PRIDE OF BARBADOS or DWARF POINCIANA

Caesalpinia pulcherrima
Size: 8 to 15 feet tall and wide
Zones: 8–11
Prefers: Full sun; average to dry, well-drained soil

Showy orange flowers and fast growth evoke the rainy tropics, but Pride of Barbados shrugs off drought. Delicate, ferny foliage softens branches armed with vicious spines, and it's a traffic-stopping shrub in full summer flower. Winter freezes kill it to the ground in its northern range, but it returns from the roots in late spring.

Philadelphus lewisii

TEXAS SAGE, TEXAS RANGER, or CENIZO

Leucophyllum frutescens
Size: 3 to 8 feet tall by 4 to 6 feet wide
Zones: 8–10
Prefers: Full sun; dry, infertile, well-drained soil

Velvety silver leaves give this evergreen shrub a moon-garden glow. Its astonishing trick of bursting into electrifying violet bloom just before a rainstorm has earned it the nickname "barometer bush." Watering won't fool it—it actually responds to humidity before and after rainstorms—so just wait for the rain.

Leucophyllum frutescens

PERENNIALS

AUTUMN SAGE or CHERRY SAGE

Salvia greggii
Size: 2 to 3 feet tall and wide
Zones: 7–9
Prefers: Full to part sun; average to dry, well-drained soil

Profuse flowering in spring and fall turns this evergreen sub-shrub into a mound of color: red, hot pink, coral, lavender, or white. A heavy hand with the pruning shears between bloom cycles ensures good flowering and reduces woodiness. Aromatic leaves release their minty fragrance at the lightest touch, so plant it along pathways. Many other salvias make excellent choices for dry gardens, including Cleveland sage (*S. clevelandii*), Mexican bush sage (*S. leucantha*), mealy blue sage (*S. farinacea*), and scarlet sage (*S. coccinea*).

BLUE FALSE INDIGO

Baptisia australis
Size: 3 to 5 feet tall and wide
Zones: 3–9
Prefers: Full to part sun; moist to dry, well-drained soil

Violet-blue flowers reminiscent of lupines adorn erect stems on this bushy perennial, followed by rattling black seedpods. Slow to establish and resentful of division or transplanting, baptisia rewards your hands-off patience after a few seasons with trouble-free, reliable growth and exuberant flowering.

BUTTERFLY WEED

Asclepias tuberosa
Size: 1 to 2 feet tall and wide
Zones: 3–9
Prefers: Full sun; average to dry, well-drained soil; suitable for the top edge of a rain garden

Like orange helipads, butterfly weed's flat-topped, showy flowers invite passing butterflies, bees, and hummingbirds to land and have lunch. Easily sprouted from seed, it needs several seasons to grow a taproot and doesn't like being moved, but the payoff comes when it's established and the long bloom season begins. Silky, parachuting seeds blow away in fall breezes.

CATMINT

Nepeta x *faassenii*
Size: 1 to 2 feet tall by 1.5 to 3 feet wide
Zones: 3–8
Prefers: Full sun to part shade; average to dry, well-drained soil

Lavender spikes stand in tall profusion over a sprawling mound of tiny, gray-green leaves from spring through summer. Fragrant foliage is too low to run your fingers through, unless planted atop a low wall, but it keeps deer from browsing.

DESERT GLOBEMALLOW or APRICOT MALLOW

Sphaeralcea ambigua
Size: 2 to 5 feet tall and wide
Zones: 6–10
Prefers: Full sun; average to dry, infertile, well-drained soil

Fuzzy, ruffled gray-green or silver leaves on wand-like, upright stems hint at globemallow's drought tolerance. In spring and summer, cup-like flowers in orange, red, or pink open along each stem, glowing in sunlight. Gravelly soil and reflected

heat make it thrive; regular irrigation, not so much. Periodic shearing benefits the plant.

DESERT MARIGOLD

Baileya multiradiata
Size: 1 to 1.5 feet tall by 2 feet wide
Zones: 7–10
Prefers: Full sun to part shade; average to dry, infertile, well-drained soil

Chrome-yellow flowers are held aloft on wiry stems over a tidy mound of wooly gray leaves, adding masses of cheerful color in spring through fall. Use gravel mulch for reflected heat and drainage, and allow some reseeding, since the plant is short lived.

DWARF FALSE INDIGO or FRAGRANT INDIGO-BUSH

Amorpha nana
Size: 1 to 3 feet tall by 1 to 2 feet wide
Zones: 4–8
Prefers: Full sun to part shade; average to dry, well-drained soil

Maroon-purple flower spikes that smell of honey and bloom all summer contrast with a cloud of delicate, ferny, green leaves on this shrubby plains native.

Baptisia australis

FALL ASTER or AROMATIC ASTER

Symphyotrichum oblongifolium

Size: 1 to 2 feet tall by 2 to 3 feet wide

Zones: 7–10

Prefers: Full to part sun; average to dry, well-drained soil

A spreading mound of small green leaves in spring and summer, fragrant but easily overlooked, is smothered each autumn with masses of purple, lavender, or lilac flowers dotted with yellow centers—a stunning display that's a siren song for bees and other pollinators. Leggier New England aster (*Symphyotrichum novae-angliae*) is a good choice in cooler regions.

GAURA or WHIRLING BUTTERFLIES

Gaura lindheimeri

Size: 3 to 5 feet tall by 1 to 3 feet wide

Zones: 5–9

Prefers: Full to part sun; average to dry, infertile, well-drained soil

Fluttery white or pink flowers range along wiry stems that nod in the breeze. Its graceful, airy habit makes it a natural choice for a cottage garden or massing in a border. Whack off spent blooms summer through fall to bring on another flush of flowers.

HUMMINGBIRD MINT

Agastache spp.

Size: 1 to 4 feet tall by 1 to 3 feet wide, varying by species

Zones: 5–10

Prefers: Full sun or afternoon shade; average to dry, well-drained soil

Sunset-hued or purple spikes of tubular flowers rise above loose mounds of minty-smelling leaves, keeping hummingbirds and sphinx moths busy all summer. Hot, humid nights are not to its liking; best suited to dry, western climates.

JUPITER'S BEARD or RED VALERIAN

Centranthus ruber

Size: 1.5 to 3 feet tall by 1 to 2 feet wide

Zones: 5–8

Prefers: Full sun to afternoon shade; average to infertile, well-drained soil

Rose-pink or dark-red clusters of fragrant flowers bloom from spring through fall atop skinny stems of gray-green, lance-shaped leaves. Native to the Mediterranean, it dislikes hot, humid summers, so it's best suited to western states. Self-seeds freely in gravelly soil.

MEXICAN HAT or PRAIRIE CONEFLOWER

Ratibida columnifera

Size: 1.5 to 3 feet tall by 1 to 1.5 feet wide

Zones: 4–9

Prefers: Full sun; average to dry, infertile, well-drained soil

Bearing blossoms like a sombrero with a drooping yellow or red-and-yellow brim atop tall, hairy stems, this prairie wildflower blooms from summer into fall. It's striking in mass plantings but lost in onesies and twosies.

PINELEAF PENSTEMON

Penstemon pinifolius

Size: 10 to 15 inches tall and wide

Zones: 4–9

Prefers: Full sun; average to dry, well-drained soil

All summer, tubular red-orange flowers are held like pennants on slim green stems. Evergreen, needle-like leaves and a tidy, mounding form make it a lovely addition to a rock garden or dry border.

'POWIS CASTLE' ARTEMISIA

Artemisia 'Powis Castle'

Size: 1.5 to 2 feet tall by 2 to 4 feet wide

Zones: 6–9

Prefers: Full to part sun; average to dry, well-drained soil

Frothy, silver-gray foliage releases a strong licorice fragrance when you rub it between your fingers, making this woody perennial unpalatable to deer. Its sprawling, mounded form offers visual cooling when planted en masse.

PURPLE CONEFLOWER

Echinacea purpurea

Size: 2 to 5 feet tall by 1.5 to 2 feet wide

Zones: 3–8

Prefers: Full to part sun; average to dry, well-drained soil

With drooping petals like pink ballerina skirts arrayed around a spiny orange disk, purple coneflower is a butterfly magnet. Let winter-browned seed heads stand in winter to feed songbirds; remaining seed easily self-sows.

Ratibida columnifera

Scutellaria wrightii

PURPLE SKULLCAP

Scutellaria wrightii
Size: 6 to 10 inches tall by 1 foot wide
Zones: 8–11
Prefers: Full to part sun; average to dry, well-drained soil

Dainty, semi-evergreen leaves contrast with masses of snapdragon-like, purple flowers that smother this tidy perennial from spring through summer. Prairie skullcap (*Scutellaria resinosa*) is a good choice in colder climates.

PURPLE TRAILING LANTANA

Lantana montevidensis
Size: 1 to 1.5 feet tall by 3 to 5 feet wide
Zones: 8–10
Prefers: Full to part sun; average to dry, well-drained soil

A sprawling cousin to shrub-sized lantanas, purple trailing lantana flowers with abandon all year, even in winter where freezes are rare. Cold weather gives the aromatic, cat's-tongue-textured leaves a burgundy tinge, harmonizing with the lilac flowers.

ROSEMARY

Rosmarinus officinalis
Size: 2 to 6 feet tall by 2 to 4 feet wide
Zones: 8–10
Prefers: Full to part sun; average to dry, well-drained soil

Stiff, pine-needle-like leaves with a strong, resinous fragrance make it unpalatable to deer. But we humans find it tasty as a seasoning and appealing in sachets, not to mention handsome in the garden. This shrubby evergreen sparkles with tiny, pale-blue flowers in winter.

RUSSIAN SAGE

Perovskia atriplicifolia
Size: 3 to 5 feet tall by 2 to 4 feet wide
Zones: 5–9
Prefers: Full sun; average to dry, well-drained soil

Like a smoky blue haze, airy flower spikes of pale lavender top this upright, fine-leaved perennial summer through fall. Fragrant, gray-green leaves resist deer browsing.

SACRED THORN-APPLE

Datura wrightii

Size: 2 to 3 feet tall by 3 to 6 feet wide

Zones: 8–10

Prefers: Full to part sun; average to dry, infertile, well-drained soil

Ghostly white, trumpet-shaped—and nearly trumpet-sized—blossoms unfurl as dusk settles over the summer garden, releasing a heady, sweet fragrance and attracting sphinx moths and other night pollinators. This coarse-leaved perennial has narcotic properties and can be deadly if nibbled, so keep it away from small children and pets.

SEA HOLLY

Eryngium spp.

Size: 1 to 3 feet tall by 1 to 2 feet wide

Zones: 2–10, depending on species

Prefers: Full sun; dry, infertile, well-drained soil

With globe-like flowers wearing pointy tutus—actually bracts, or modified leaves—sea holly adds spiky, thistly drama to the dry garden. Tall, branching stems hold up the unusual steely blue or purple flowers, which are easily grown from seed provided you don't coddle them.

THREADLEAF COREOPSIS

Coreopsis verticillata

Size: 1.5 to 2 feet tall and wide

Zones: 3–9

Prefers: Full to part sun; average to dry, well-drained soil

Yellow, raggedy-edged flowers glow, summer through fall, like miniature suns amid needle-thin, emerald leaves. Deadheading encourages a new flush of blooms.

WILD BUCKWHEAT or SULFUR BUCKWHEAT

Eriogonum umbellatum

Size: 6 to 12 inches tall by 1 to 3 feet wide

Zones: 4–10

Prefers: Full sun; dry, infertile, well-drained soil

Forest-green leaves are blanketed in spring by golden, button-like flowers that fade to rusty tones by late summer. This mat-forming, western native appreciates low humidity and poor, dry soil. Numerous other species are also available.

Bouteloua gracilis
'Blonde Ambition'

YARROW

Achillea millefolium

Size: 2 to 3 feet tall and wide

Zones: 3–9

Prefers: Full sun to dappled shade; average to dry, well-drained soil

Flat parasols of tiny, clustered, white flowers are held above feathery foliage. In hot climates, it works as a ferny groundcover in dappled shade. Numerous cultivars offer yellow, white, candy-pink, and rusty-red flowers.

GRASSES AND SEDGES
BAMBOO MUHLY

Muhlenbergia dumosa

Size: 3 to 6 feet tall by 3 to 5 feet wide

Zones: 8–10

Prefers: Full sun to dappled shade; average to dry, well-drained soil

This upright, vase-shaped, clumping grass with feathery foliage billows in summer breezes like a chartreuse cloud. Its pettable texture, yellow-green coloring, and absolute toughness make this a dry-garden gem.

BIG MUHLY or LINDHEIMER MUHLY

Muhlenbergia lindheimeri

Size: 2 to 4 feet tall and wide

Zones: 7–11

Prefers: Full to part sun; average to dry soil

Fine, blue-green, arching leaves are topped in fall with 6-foot wands of pale-mauve flowers that age to silver-blond. For smaller spaces or to mix it up, try Gulf muhly (*Muhlenbergia capillaris*), with fall flowers that create a haze of cotton-candy pink.

'BLONDE AMBITION' BLUE GRAMA

Bouteloua gracilis 'Blonde Ambition'

Size: 2 to 3 feet tall and wide

Zones: 3–10

Prefers: Full sun; average to dry, well-drained soil

This bunching, blue-green grass blooms summer through fall with a fireworks-like explosion of pale, comb-shaped flowers held horizontally like flirtatiously winking eyelashes.

DWARF MAIDEN GRASS

Miscanthus sinensis 'Adagio'

Size: 3 to 4 feet tall and wide

Zones: 5–9

Prefers: Full to part sun; average, well-drained soil

Tasseled, pinkish tan plumes rise in fall above mounded, green leaves, which are streaked with hot pink and yellow in cooler weather. Lovely as a specimen plant or massed in a border.

LITTLE BLUESTEM

Schizachyrium scoparium
Size: 2 to 4 feet tall by 1 foot wide
Zones: 3–9
Prefers: Full sun; average to dry soil;
suitable for rain gardens

Fine-textured, blue-green leaves
are topped in late summer by fluffy,
pinkish-purple seed heads. With cooler
weather, seed heads fade to silver,
and foliage takes on a burnished,
russet hue.

MEXICAN FEATHERGRASS

Nassella tenuissima
Size: 1 foot tall by 1 to 1.5 feet wide
Zones: 7–11
Prefers: Full sun to part shade; average
to dry, well-drained soil

Chartreuse, vase-shaped foliage is
topped in spring or summer (depending
on climate) with feathery blond blooms
that dance on the lightest breeze.
Aggressive self-seeding means it
can be invasive in some regions, but
for the rest, it's a graceful, tough-as-
nails beauty.

NORTHERN SEA OATS or INLAND SEA OATS

Chasmanthium latifolium
Size: 2 to 3 feet tall by 1 to 2.5 feet wide
Zones: 3–9
Prefers: Full sun to shade; moist to dry
soil; suitable for rain gardens

Fresh, apple-green leaves on arching
stems emerge in spring. By early
summer dangling, oat-like seed heads
form, first green and then fading
to tan. Highly ornamental in shade
and in rain gardens, this grass seeds
out aggressively with extra water,
especially in gravel.

PINE MUHLY

Muhlenbergia dubia
Size: 2 to 3 feet tall by 2 to 4 feet wide
Zones: 7–10
Prefers: Full sun; average to dry,
well-drained soil

With a symmetrical form like an
exploding firework, exceptional
drought tolerance, and a relatively
small size, this fine-leaved grass
is a star in the dry garden. Pinkish
tan blooms appear in late summer
through fall.

PRAIRIE DROPSEED

Sporobolus heterolepis

Size: 1 to 2 feet tall and wide
Zones: 3–9
Prefers: Full sun; average to dry, well-drained soil

Graceful, fine-textured, mounding leaves start out bright green and turn to burnt orange in fall. Airy, silvery-pink seed heads in late summer create a sparkling haze above the foliage.

SEDGE

Carex spp.

Size: 4 to 12 inches tall and wide
Zones: 3–11, depending on species
Prefers: Full sun to shade; average to dry soil

Short, grassy tufts make a meadowy alternative to lawn and are especially useful in dry shade where turf grass won't grow. Favorites include Berkeley (*Carex divulsa*), Texas (*C. texensis*), Appalachian (*C. appalachica*), and Penn (*C. pensylvanica*) sedges.

WOODY LILIES, SUCCULENTS, AND CACTI
'ANGELINA' SEDUM

Sedum rupestre 'Angelina'

Size: 6 inches tall by 1 to 3 feet wide
Zones: 3–9
Prefers: Full sun to bright shade; average to dry, well-drained soil

Soft, needle-like, chartreuse foliage spills across the ground like a puddle of sunshine. Evergreen, fleshy leaves turn orange in fall. Works beautifully in containers and rock gardens.

ARTICHOKE AGAVE

Agave parryi var. *truncata*

Size: 1 to 2 feet tall by 1.5 to 2.5 feet wide
Zones: 8–11
Prefers: Full to part sun; dry, infertile, well-drained soil

Symmetrically arrayed layers of tightly held, blue-gray leaves form this small but stunning agave. A slow grower that rarely pups (makes offsets), it's well suited to containers and small gardens.

BEAKED YUCCA or BIG BEND YUCCA

Yucca rostrata

Size: 6 to 12 feet tall by 4 to 5 feet wide
Zones: 5–11
Prefers: Full sun; dry, infertile, well-drained soil

Like a Koosh ball of strappy, flexible leaves, this dramatic yucca shimmers in the breeze. It's slow growing but eventually forms a shaggy trunk, elevating the sphere of foliage to play against the blue sky. The cultivar 'Sapphire Skies' has especially beautiful powder-blue leaves.

BULBINE

Bulbine frutescens

Size: 10 to 18 inches tall by 1.5 to
3 feet wide

Zones: 8–11

Prefers: Full to part sun; average to dry,
well-drained soil

With grassy, fleshy leaves that grow
in widening clumps, this South
African native makes a lush, evergreen
groundcover in mild-winter climates.
Light-catching, wand-like flower spikes
in soft-orange or yellow rise above the
foliage from spring through fall.

CLARET CUP CACTUS or SCARLET HEDGEHOG CACTUS

Echinocereus coccineus

Size: 6 to 24 inches tall, clustering
2 to 3 feet wide

Zones: 5–9

Prefers: Full sun; dry, infertile,
well-drained soil

White spines the length of sewing
needles make a fine web across the
ribbed, upright stems of this spreading,
cold-tolerant cactus. In spring, a bold
profusion of scarlet or orange-red
flowers appears.

'COLOR GUARD' YUCCA

Yucca filamentosa 'Color Guard'

Size: 1.5 to 2 feet tall by 2 to 3 feet
wide; 4- to 6-foot bloom spike

Zones: 4–10

Prefers: Full sun to afternoon sun;
average to dry, well-drained soil

Snazzy yellow-and-green stripes,
its relatively small size, and an open,
spherical form make this yucca a
garden standout. Its sharp-tipped,
smooth-edged leaves flex and bend,
so it won't draw (too much) blood
should you accidentally back into it.

GHOST PLANT

Graptopetalum paraguayense

Size: 6 to 12 inches tall, clustering
2 to 3 feet wide

Zones: 7–10

Prefers: Full sun to bright shade;
average to dry, well-drained soil

Fleshy rosettes colored taupe, gray-
blue, and dusky pink cluster in
widening clumps and eventually
cascade on long stems, making this
a wonderful container plant.

Echinocereus coccineus

Agave havardiana

GOPHER PLANT

Euphorbia rigida

Size: 1 to 2 feet tall by 1 to 3 feet wide

Zones: 7–10

Prefers: Full to part sun; average to dry, well-drained soil

Tidy, blue-green leaves on upturned stems make this evergreen lovely in all seasons. But in spring, when chartreuse flowers and bracts open at the tips of each stem, it seems to vibrate with sunny color. Cut back the long stems after flowers go to seed, and wear gloves and goggles to protect skin and eyes from an irritating latex sap that oozes from any cut.

HARVARD AGAVE

Agave havardiana

Size: 2 to 3 feet tall by 3 to 4 feet wide

Zones: 6–10

Prefers: Full sun to bright shade; dry, infertile, well-drained soil

Stiff, triangular leaves of gray-blue are arrayed like a stylized setting sun. With small teeth along each leaf and a contrasting black spine at the end, this plant has a painful bite. Just give it plenty of room and enjoy its architectural beauty, which is particularly dramatic against billowing grasses.

HENS AND CHICKS

Sempervivum tectorum

Size: 3 to 6 inches tall, clustering to 6 to 12 inches wide

Zones: 3–11

Prefers: Full sun to bright shade; average to dry, well-drained soil

Fleshy green rosettes tipped with purple resemble ever-blooming flowers. Its common name comes from its habit of making numerous offsets— that is, baby plants—that cluster around the mother plant like newly hatched chicks.

PALELEAF YUCCA

Yucca pallida

Size: 1 to 2 feet tall and wide; bloom spike to 5 feet

Zones: 6–10

Prefers: Full sun to shade; average to dry, infertile, well-drained soil

With twisting, blue-gray leaves and a surprising tolerance for shade, this little yucca shines no matter where you plant it. Bell-shaped white flowers atop long stems appear in spring.

PRICKLY PEAR

Opuntia spp.

Size: 3 inches to 10 feet tall by 2 to 10 feet wide, depending on species
Zones: 3–10, depending on species
Prefers: Full sun to afternoon sun; dry, infertile, well-drained soil

With paddle-shaped stems that may be round or elongated, spiny or smooth, ground-hugging or hedge-forming, *Opuntia* species are native to nearly every U.S. state. Their bold, whimsical forms are topped with jewel-bright flowers in spring or summer. Check hardiness, as some species are more cold tolerant than others.

RED YUCCA

Hesperaloe parviflora

Size: 2 to 3 feet tall by 2 to 4 feet wide; bloom spike to 6 feet
Zones: 7–10
Prefers: Full to part sun; average to dry, well-drained soil

It's not really a yucca, and its flowers aren't red but rose-pink. Dense, fibrous evergreen leaves grow in spreading clumps and support long, arching bloom stalks spring through fall. The masses of tubular flowers are hummingbird (and deer) bait.

SOAP ALOE

Aloe maculata

Size: 18 inches tall by 18 to 24 inches wide; bloom spike to 3 feet
Zones: 8–11
Prefers: Full sun to part shade; average to dry, well-drained soil

From a rosette of star-shaped, fleshy leaves spattered with creamy freckles, intermittent bloom spikes emerge, with tubular red-orange flowers that attract bees and hummingbirds. Soap aloe pups prolifically, sending out baby plants via running stems; these can be snipped off to keep a solitary specimen or allowed to form a spreading cluster.

TEXAS NOLINA or BEARGRASS

Nolina texana

Size: 1.5 to 2.5 feet tall by 3 to 4 feet wide
Zones: 7–10
Prefers: Full sun to shade; average to dry, infertile, well-drained soil

Evergreen, spaghetti-slender leaves form a languid mound on level ground or cascade down a slope. In spring or summer, stout flower stems bearing creamy flowers nestle amid the leaves.

Chamaerops humilis var. *cerifera*

WHALE'S TONGUE AGAVE

Agave ovatifolia

Size: 3 to 4 feet tall by 4 to 6 feet wide

Zones: 7–9

Prefers: Full sun to dappled shade; average to dry, infertile, well-drained soil

With powder-blue leaves that look wide enough to swallow Jonah, whale's tongue resembles a big dusky-blue rose. Solitary and non-pupping, this stunning agave appreciates afternoon shade in the hottest climates.

WHEELER SOTOL or DESERT SPOON

Dasylirion wheeleri

Size: 4 to 6 feet tall by 3 to 4 feet wide

Zones: 6–10

Prefers: Full sun; dry, infertile, well-drained soil

Blue-gray, strappy leaves, each edged with hundreds of tiny, light-catching teeth, are held in a perfect sphere. Wind makes the leaves shimmer and dance.

PALMS AND CYCADS

MEDITERRANEAN FAN PALM

Chamaerops humilis

Size: Very slow growing to 10 to 20 feet tall and wide

Zones: 8–11

Prefers: Full sun to dappled shade; average to dry, well-drained soil

Elegant, long-fingered fans of evergreen leaves give this drought-tolerant palm a tropical look. Eventually, slowly, it grows multiple trunks. Water regularly to establish. A silver-blue variety, *Chamaerops humilis* var. *cerifera*, is also available.

SAGO PALM

Cycas revoluta

Size: Very slow growing to 10 to 12 feet tall by 8 to 10 feet wide

Zones: 8–10

Prefers: Full sun to shade; average to dry, well-drained soil

Sago palm hasn't much changed since the age of dinosaurs. Arching fronds of stiff, needle-like leaves eventually form a bushy, forest-green clump atop a short trunk.

SAW PALMETTO

Serenoa repens

Size: Slow growing to 4 to 6 feet tall
and wide

Zones: 8–11

Prefers: Full sun to dappled shade;
moist to dry, well-drained soil

Windmilling fans of silver-green leaves
resemble a mound of jazz hands.
Eventually it forms multiple trunks.
Razor-sharp stems require respectful
spacing from paths or patios. Water
regularly to establish.

GROUNDCOVERS

LAMB'S EAR

Stachys byzantina

Size: 4 to 12 inches tall by 1 to
3 feet wide

Zones: 4–8

Prefers: Full sun to bright shade;
average to dry, well-drained soil

Pettable, velvety leaves of silver or
silver-green make an attractive, light-
reflecting mat. Give it afternoon shade
in hot climates.

LEADWORT PLUMBAGO

Ceratostigma plumbaginoides

Size: 6 to 12 inches tall by 1 to
1.5 feet wide

Zones: 5–9

Prefers: Full sun to part shade; average,
well-drained soil

Brilliant blue flowers set off by reddish
brown calyces (the papery outer part
of the flower) bloom in late summer
and fall atop a mat of green leaves that
turn a bronzed red in winter. Readily
spreads via underground stems.

PINKS or CHEDDAR PINKS

Dianthus gratianopolitanus

Size: 6 to 12 inches tall by 1 to
2 feet wide

Zones: 3–9

Prefers: Full to part sun; average,
well-drained soil

Forming a mat of narrow, blue-green
leaves, this low-growing perennial is
handsome in bloom or out. In spring
it's carpeted with magenta, pale-pink,
or red flowers, whose ragged edges
look as if cut out with pinking shears.
Plant atop a low wall or in a container
to enjoy the clove-like fragrance.

SILVER CARPET

Dymondia margaretae

Size: 1 to 3 inches tall by 1 to
2 feet wide

Zones: 9–11

Prefers: Full sun to light shade; dry,
infertile, well-drained soil

A true ground-hugger, silver carpet
makes a spreading lake of silver green.
Narrow leaves curl slightly along the
edges to flash their white undersides,
adding more reflective sparkle. Yellow
flowers are tucked among the leaves in
summer. Water regularly to establish,
then rarely.

SILVER PONYFOOT

Dichondra argentea

Size: 3 to 4 inches tall by 3 to
4 feet wide

Zones: 8–10

Prefers: Full sun to light shade; average
to dry, well-drained soil

Like elfin, silver-green lily pads, the
leaves of silver ponyfoot cluster along
spreading stems. Especially nice atop
walls or in containers where it can
cascade over the edge.

ST. JOHN'S WORT or AARON'S BEARD

Hypericum calycinum

Size: 1 to 1.5 feet tall by 1.5 to
2 feet wide

Zones: 5–7

Prefers: Full sun to part shade; average
to dry, well-drained soil

Showy, banana-yellow flowers with a
fiber-optic spray of stamens stand out
in summer against handsome green
leaves. Evergreen in warmer regions.
Spreads via underground runners.

TURKISH SPEEDWELL

Veronica liwanensis

Size: 1 to 3 inches tall by 1 to
2 feet wide

Zones: 4–8

Prefers: Full sun to light shade; average
to dry, infertile, well-drained soil

Glossy leaves form a spreading mat,
which is transformed in spring with
a haze of blue-violet flowers atop
short stems. This is a good choice to
place between stepping stones and
in rock gardens.

WINECUP or PURPLE POPPY MALLOW

Callirhoe involucrata

Size: 6 to 12 inches tall by 1 to 3 feet wide

Zones: 4–8

Prefers: Full sun; average to dry, well-drained soil

Drink your fill of this charming groundcover with magenta flowers that glow like stained glass in sunlight. In hot climates, it goes dormant in summer but reappears reliably in spring.

WOOLLY STEMODIA

Stemodia lanata

Size: 4 to 6 inches tall by 2 to 3 feet wide

Zones: 8–10

Prefers: Full to part sun; average to dry, infertile, well-drained soil

A mat of silvery white leaves cascades nicely over slopes or walls and quickly spreads via underground stems. In late spring and summer, tiny lavender flowers sparkle amid the foliage.

VINES
BUTTERFLY VINE or GALLINITA

Mascagnia macroptera

Size: 15 to 20 feet tall and wide

Zones: 8–10

Prefers: Full to part sun; average to dry, well-drained soil

Pinwheel-like flowers of lemon yellow smother this handsome evergreen vine in summer and fall. Seed heads, which appear alongside the flowers in summer, resemble papery butterflies that start out chartreuse and fade to tan.

CORAL HONEYSUCKLE

Lonicera sempervirens

Size: 8 to 20 feet tall and wide

Zones: 4–9

Prefers: Full to part sun; average, well-drained soil

Tubular pinkish-red flowers dangle like chandelier earrings amid shiny, oval, semi-evergreen leaves. Flowers lack fragrance, but the tradeoff is a well-mannered, noninvasive vine. Hummingbirds love it.

Stemodia lanata

Bignonia capreolata
'Tangerine Beauty'

CORAL VINE or QUEEN'S WREATH

Antigonon leptopus
Size: 8 to 40 feet tall and wide
Zones: 8–11
Prefers: Full sun to part shade; average to dry, well-drained soil

With heart-shaped green leaves and cascades of deep-pink flowers, this twining, high-climbing vine seems ready-made for Valentine's Day. The showy flowers are instead a late summer and fall treat.

LADY BANKS ROSE

Rosa banksiae 'Lutea'
Size: 12 to 20 feet tall and wide
Zones: 7–10
Prefers: Full sun; average, well-drained soil

Frilly yellow flowers in spring or early summer along cascading green stems make a romantic, lightly fragrant bower. Thornless canes and evergreen leaves (in mild-winter climates) are a bonus. Site carefully, as it is capable of swallowing a shed whole.

SNAPDRAGON VINE

Maurandella antirrhiniflora
Size: 3 to 10 feet tall and wide
Zones: 8–10
Prefers: Full to part sun; average to dry, well-drained soil

Snapdragon-shaped purple flowers bloom all summer along stems of small, English ivy-like leaves. Makes a dainty, well-behaved vine for a fence or mailbox.

'TANGERINE BEAUTY' CROSSVINE

Bignonia capreolata 'Tangerine Beauty'
Size: 20 to 30 feet tall and wide
Zones: 5–9
Prefers: Full sun to dappled shade; average to dry, well-drained soil

Festive, trumpet-shaped orange flowers herald spring or summer's arrival and attract hummingbirds. Evergreen leaves (in mild-winter climates) keep this vigorous climber attractive all year.

BULBS
BEARDED IRIS

Iris germanica hybrids
Size: 8 inches to 4 feet tall by 1 to 2 feet wide, depending on cultivar
Zones: 3–10
Prefers: Full to part sun; average to dry, well-drained soil

Ruffled, showy flowers stand tall above sword-shaped leaves in spring or early summer. Numerous cultivars offer a rainbow of colors, including purple, peach, yellow, and white. Divide every 3 to 5 years for best blooms. Diminutive reticulated iris (*Iris reticulata*) is also a good choice.

GARLIC CHIVES

Allium tuberosum
Size: 1 to 1.5 feet tall by 1 to 2 feet wide
Zones: 3–9
Prefers: Full sun to dappled shade;
average to dry, well-drained soil

Onion-scented, grassy, edible leaves
send up tall stems of starry white
flowers in late summer—like a delayed
Fourth of July sparkler. Bees adore
it; deer do not. It readily seeds out in
gravelly soil.

GRAPE HYACINTH

Muscari spp.
Size: 4 to 12 inches tall by 3 to
6 inches wide
Zones: 4–8
Prefers: Full sun to part shade; average
to dry, well-drained soil

Violet-blue flowers are held tightly on
short flower spikes in spring. Lanky,
grassy leaves go dormant in summer
but reappear in fall.

'LUCIFER' CROCOSMIA

Crocosmia 'Lucifer'
Size: 2 to 4 feet tall by 1 to 2 feet wide
Zones: 7–9
Prefers: Full sun to part shade; average
to dry, well-drained soil

Tall, sword-like, deep green leaves
contrast with devilishly red flower
clusters in summer. This is a
showstopper of rich color.

OXBLOOD LILY

Rhodophiala bifida
Size: 10 to 16 inches tall by 6 to
12 inches wide
Zones: 7–10
Prefers: Full sun to dappled shade;
average to dry, well-drained soil

Red, amaryllis-like flowers with yellow
stamens pop up seemingly overnight
with the first fall rains to announce
summer's end. Leaves appear
after the flowers fade and remain
through winter.

RAIN LILY

Zephyranthes grandiflora
Size: 6 to 10 inches tall by 1 to
1.5 feet wide
Zones: 8–11
Prefers: Full to part sun; average to dry,
well-drained soil

True to its name, rain lily blooms
immediately after a summer downpour.
Cotton-candy-pink flowers appear
en masse above strappy, glossy
green leaves that remain through
the winter. Don't bother trying to
fool zephyranthes with a sprinkling
from the watering can; it only flowers
for rain, a sweet celebration. White-
flowering *Zephyranthes candida*, hardy
to zone 7, is another good choice.

Allium tuberosum

Gaillardia pulchella

ANNUALS
CALIFORNIA POPPY

Eschscholzia californica

Size: 1 to 1.5 feet tall and wide

Zones: Annual; perennial in some climates

Prefers: Full sun; average to dry, infertile, well-drained soil

Cup-like, golden-orange flowers unfurl from pointed buds in spring or in summer in cooler climates. Finely textured, ferny leaves are gray-green.

DAHLBERG DAISY

Thymophylla tenuiloba

Size: 6 to 12 inches tall and wide

Zones: Annual

Prefers: Full sun; average to dry, well-drained soil

A sunny smattering of yellow daisies tops lacy green foliage, summer through fall. Nice for containers, rock gardens, and dry borders.

INDIAN BLANKET or FIREWHEEL

Gaillardia pulchella

Size: 1 to 2 feet tall and wide

Zones: Annual

Prefers: Full sun; average to dry, infertile, well-drained soil

Festive, sawtooth-edged flower disks of red and yellow bloom above hairy leaves in summer.

NARROWLEAF ZINNIA

Zinnia angustifolia

Size: 8 to 12 inches tall by 1 to 2 feet wide

Zones: Annual

Prefers: Full sun; average to dry, well-drained soil

Profuse orange flowers sizzle all summer atop a mound of narrow leaves. For visual cooling, a white cultivar is available too.

acknowledgments

For sharing inspirational water-saving gardens with me, grateful thanks to
Curt Arnette, Noelle Johnson, John Kuzma, Steve Martino, Rebecca Sams,
and Christine Ten Eyck. Thanks also to Lauren Springer Ogden for her
mentorship and for leading by example. To my editorial and design team
at Ten Speed Press, Kaitlin Ketchum, Kara Plikaitis, and copyeditor Kristi
Hein, thanks for giving my words and images a polish and a beautiful frame.
To friends and strangers who opened their garden gates and invited me in,
thank you for the inspiration and photo ops. And to my fellow shutterbugs
who've shared images with me, I owe you one. Love and thanks to David,
Aaron, and Julia, my fellow adventurers and my reason to come home.
And finally, enormous gratitude to readers of my blog, Digging, where it
all began.

A desert garden bursts into colorful bloom in the spring.

recommended resources

additional reading

Artful Rainwater Design: Creative Ways to Manage Stormwater. Stuart Echols and Eliza Pennypacker, 2015. Washington, D.C.: Island Press.

Designing with Succulents. Debra Lee Baldwin, 2007. Portland, OR: Timber Press.

Drip Irrigation for Every Landscape and All Climates, 2nd ed. Robert Kourik, 2009. Occidental, CA: Metamorphic Press.

The Gardener's Guide to Cactus: The 100 Best Paddles, Barrels, Columns, and Globes. Scott Calhoun, 2012. Portland, OR: Timber Press.

Hellstrip Gardening: Create a Paradise between the Sidewalk and the Curb. Evelyn Hadden, 2014. Portland, OR: Timber Press.

The Hot Garden: Landscape Design for the Desert Southwest. Scott Calhoun, 2009. Tucson, AZ: Rio Nuevo Press.

Lawn Gone! Low-Maintenance, Sustainable, Attractive Alternatives for Your Yard. Pam Penick, 2013. Berkeley, CA: Ten Speed Press.

Rainwater Harvesting for Drylands and Beyond, Volume 1, 2nd Edition: Guiding Principles to Welcome Rain into Your Life and Landscape. Brad Lancaster, 2013. Tucson, AZ: Rainsource Press.

Small Green Roofs: Low-Tech Options for Greener Living. Nigel Dunnett, Dusty Gedge, John Little, and Edmund C. Snodgrass, 2011. Portland, OR: Timber Press.

Sunset Western Landscaping Book. Kathleen Norris Brenzel, ed., 2006. Birmingham, AL: Oxmoor House.

The Undaunted Garden: Planting for Weather-Resilient Beauty, 2nd ed. Lauren Springer Ogden, 2011. Golden, CO: Fulcrum Publishing.

Waterwise Plants for Sustainable Gardens: 200 Drought-Tolerant Choices for All Climates. Lauren Springer Ogden and Scott Ogden, 2011. Portland, OR: Timber Press.

Yard Full of Sun: The Story of a Gardener's Obsession that Got a Little Out of Hand. Scott Calhoun, 2005. Tucson, AZ: Rio Nuevo.

useful websites

clean-water.uwex.edu/pubs/pdf/rgmanual.pdf

greywateraction.org

harvestingrainwater.com

penick.net/digging/?p=3376

plants.usda.gov/java/noxiousDriver

wateruseitwisely.com

wildflower.org/plants

photography and design credits

Photography by the author except where noted.

Front cover (bottom) and pages 52, 67 (top), 107 (right), 128, 140, 169 (bottom right), 193 (right), 197, Design: Pam Penick, Austin, TX.

Pages i, vi, 100, 107 (left), 155 (top), Desert Botanical Garden, Phoenix, AZ.

Pages iv, 20-21, Chanticleer, Wayne, PA.

Pages 2, 176 (top left), Garden of Reuben Muñoz, Riverside, CA. Photos: Reuben Muñoz/Rancho Reubidoux.

Pages 5, 103 (right), 139, 188 (right), 234, Denver Botanic Gardens, Denver, CO. Photo page 5: Les Parks.

Pages 7, 67 (bottom), 124, Garden of Curt and Melisa Arnette, Austin, TX. Design: Curt Arnette/Sitio Design.

Pages 9, 11, 95 (bottom left), 176 (bottom), Lakewood Garden, Austin, TX. Design: Curt Arnette/Sitio Design.

Pages 12-13, Garden of Ted and Nancy Dobson, Eugene, OR. Design and photos: Mosaic Gardens.

Pages 14-15, 160 (left), Quartz Mountain Garden, Paradise Valley, AZ. Design: Steve Martino.

Pages 17-18, 47, Garden of Christine Ten Eyck, Austin, TX.

Pages 22-24, 95 (bottom right), Garden of John Kuzma, Portland, OR. Design: Sean Hogan/Cistus Design.

Pages 25-28, 106, 169 (top right), 186, Scottsdale Xeriscape Demonstration Garden, Scottsdale, AZ. Design: Christine Ten Eyck.

Pages 29, 134 (top left), Garden of Tamara Paulat, Portland, OR.

Pages 30, 70 (left), 120, Mirador Garden, Austin, TX. Design: Curt Arnette/ Sitio Design.

Pages 32 (middle), 112, Garden of Scott Weber, Portland, OR.

Pages 32 (right), 188 (left), Garden of Dugie and David Graham, Austin, TX.

Page 34 (top), Garden of Paul and Kay Passmore, Dallas, TX.

Pages 34 (bottom), 48 (bottom right), 94, Rollingwood City Hall Waterwise Garden, Austin, TX. Design: Scott Ogden & Lauren Springer Ogden/Plant-Driven Design and Patrick Kirwin.

Page 35, Garden of Karen Lantz, Houston, TX.

Page 36, Garden of Ruthie Burrus, Austin, TX.

Pages 39, 104, 109 (left), 132, 134 (bottom right), 136, 162, 172, 175, 198, Lady Bird Johnson Wildflower Center, Austin, TX.

Pages 41 (top), 49 (top right), Design and photos: Suzanne Edney/Custom Landscapes, Apex, NC.

Page 41 (bottom), Evergreen Brick Works, Toronto, Ontario.

Page 42, Maplewood Mall, Maplewood, MN. Design: Ramsey-Washington Metro Watershed District and Barr Engineering. Photo: Evelyn J. Hadden.

Page 44 (top), Perot Museum of Nature and Science, Dallas, TX.

Page 44 (bottom left), High Point neighborhood, Seattle, WA. Photo: Stuart P. Echols.

Page 44 (bottom right), Siskiyou Green Street Project, Portland, OR.

Page 48 (bottom left), Garden of Noelle Johnson, Phoenix, AZ. Photo: Noelle Johnson.

Pages 49 (top left), 113, 134 (bottom left), New York Botanical Garden, New York, NY.

Page 51, Garden of Craig Helfrich, Austin, TX. Design: Pam Penick.

Page 54, Garden of Jeff Pavlat, Austin, TX.

Page 56, Photo: Sheryl Williams.

Page 57, Garden of Bruce Wakefield and Jerry Grossnickle, Portland, OR.

Pages 58, 152, Garden of James David and Gary Peese, Austin, TX.

Pages 61 (top), 155 (bottom left and right), 156, Garden of JJ De Sousa, Portland, OR.

Page 61 (bottom), Garden of Ray Hendricks, Austin, TX. Design: Fertile Ground Gardens.

Pages 62, 167 (left), 176 (top right), Lotusland, Santa Barbara, CA.

Page 65, Garden of David Morello, Houston, TX. Design: David Morello Garden Enterprises.

Pages 68, 77, 126, 164, Garden of Lori Daul. Photos 68, 77: Lori Daul.

Page 73, Garden of Charlotte Warren, Austin, TX. Design: Curt Arnette/Sitio Design.

Page 80 (right), Photo: Marc Opperman.

Page 82, Garden of Ann and Robin Matthews, Austin, TX.

Page 84, Gullett Elem. School teaching garden, Austin, TX. Design: Patrick Smith.

Pages 87, 177, ASU Polytechnic Campus, Mesa, AZ. Design: Ten Eyck Landscape Architects.

Page 98, Juniper Level Botanic Garden, Plant Delights Nursery, Raleigh, NC.

Pages 99, 178 (right), Design: Jill Nokes, Austin, TX.

Pages 102, 134 (top right), 145, Civano, Tucson, AZ.

Page 103 (left), Design: Curtis & Windham Architects, Houston, TX.

Pages 108, 173, Bedrock Gardens, Lee, NH.

Pages 109 (right), 146, Wave Hill, New York, NY.

Page 110, Antique Rose Emporium, San Antonio, TX.

Pages 111, 190, Garden of Jenny and David Stocker, Austin, TX.

Pages 114, 117, Design and photos: Korina Qu Petrozzi/The Plant Nerd, Inc., Huntington Beach, CA.

Pages 116, 185 (left), Garden of Michael McDowell, Plano, TX. Photo page 185: Michael McDowell.

Page 118, Garden of Jill Nokes, Austin, TX.

Page 121, Design: Environmental Survey Consulting, Austin, TX.

Page 123 (left), Photo: Denise Maher, Venice, CA.

Page 123 (right), Design: Floradora and BuenoLuna, Walnut Creek, CA.

Page 129, Garden of Andrea Testa-Vought, Palo Alto, CA. Design: Bernard Trainor.

Pages 130-131, 180 (right), Garden of Bruce Baldwin and Colleen Jamison, Austin, TX.

Pages 142-143, Garden of Tait Moring, Austin, TX.

Page 144 (left), Design: Noelle Johnson, Phoenix, AZ.

Page 144 (right), Bella Madrona Garden, Portland, OR.

Page 150 (top left), Redenta's Garden, Arlington, TX.

Page 150 (top right, bottom right), Antique Rose Emporium, Brenham, TX.

Pages 157, 161, Garden of Loree Bohl, Portland, OR.

Pages 158-159, Garden of Linda Ernst, Portland, OR.

Page 160 (middle), Garden of Syd Teague, Austin, TX.

Page 163, Garden of Christopher Mello, Asheville, NC.

Page 166, Garden of Trey and Brianne Denton/Blue Lotus, Dallas, TX.

Page 169 (top left), Garden of Scott Meyer, Austin, TX.

Page 169 (bottom left), Garden of Bobbie Tsukahara and Gil Starkey, Austin, TX.

Pages 170, 195, Westwind Farm Studio, Portland, OR. Design: John Greenlee.

Page 174, Olbrich Botanical Gardens, Madison, WI.

Page 178 (left), Design: Curt Arnette/ Sitio Design.

Page 179, Lurie Garden, Chicago, IL. Design: Piet Oudolf.

Pages 180 (left), 194, Garden of Lucinda Hutson, Austin, TX.

Page 181, Ruth Bancroft Garden, Walnut Creek, CA. Photo: Marilyn B. Hughes.

Page 182, Garden of Lynne Blackman, Del Mar, CA. Photo: Steve Gunther.

Page 184, Bloedel Reserve, Bainbridge Island, WA.

Pages 185 (right), 193 (left), Garden of Tom Spencer, Austin, TX.

Page 223, Design: Steve Martino, Paradise Valley, AZ.

Page 225, Garden of Tom Ellison, Austin, TX.

index

Published in the United States by Ten Speed Press,
an imprint of the Crown Publishing Group, a division
of Penguin Random House LLC, New York.
www.crownpublishing.com
www.tenspeed.com

Ten Speed Press and the Ten Speed Press colophon are
registered trademarks of Penguin Random House LLC.

All photographs, except as noted on pages 226–228,
are copyright to the author.

Some photos previously appeared on www.penick.net.

Library of Congress Cataloging-in-Publication Data
Penick, Pam, author.
The water-saving garden / by Pam Penick.—First edition.
pages cm
1. Xeriscaping. 2. Water conservation. 3. Drought-tolerant
plants. I. Title.
SB475.83.P46 2016
635.9—dc23
                2015025964

Trade paperback ISBN: 978-1-60774-793-2
eBook ISBN: 978-1-60774-794-9

Printed in China

Design by Kara Plikaitis

10 9 8 7 6 5 4 3 2 1

First Edition